SHA

Shat

Written by:

Copyright 2012

Cover art: Valerie Bowen

Edited by: Gail Holland

Published by: V. J. Bowen

Printed and Distributed in U.S.A.

Disclosure

The characters, events and some locations portrayed in this book are fictitious products of the author's mind. Any similarity to real persons, living or dead is coincidental and not intended by the author.

Note from the author

This novel is based on a true story. Although the names of the victim and the families remain anonymous, the events are real. The entire story is from the memory of the victim.

Other novels by Valerie Bowen

For the Sake of Amelia series
Tormented
Inhibition
Retribution

Mind of a Madman series
Evil Unleashed
Evil Stalks
Evil Redemption

Newly released
The Drifter

Coming soon
The Enchanted Oasis

DEDICATION

This book is dedicated to the many victims of psychological abuse. Although the scars cannot be seen, they do exist. It's my hope; all victims of mental abuse can find the strength to leave their abuser before the unspeakable occurs.

Bullying a loved one is just as unacceptable as a child being bullied at school. Stand up for the rights of psychological victims. Take note and listen to the hateful words coming from the mouths of family and friends. Know hateful words can damage a soul and remember, it just might be your words that may cause the victim's demise.

Acknowledgements:

Although I'm the author of this novel, there are a few people that helped along the way. The victim who was willing to share her story because, without her words the novel never would have come to light. Gail Holland: for her fine editing skills and her willingness to go above and beyond.

Table of Contents

Chapter 1:
Chapter 2:
Chapter 3:
Chapter 4:
Chapter 5:
Chapter 6:
Chapter 7:
Chapter 8:
Chapter 9:
Chapter 10:
Chapter 11:
Chapter 12:
Chapter 13:
Chapter 14:
Chapter 15:
Chapter 16:
Chapter 17:
Chapter 18:
Chapter 19:
Chapter 20:
Chapter 21:
Chapter 22:
Chapter 23:
Chapter 24:
Chapter 25:
Chapter 26:
Chapter 27:

Table of Contents Continued

Chapter 28:
Chapter 29:
Chapter 30:
Chapter 31:
Chapter 32:
Chapter 33:
Chapter 34:
Chapter 35:
Chapter 37:
Chapter 38:
Chapter 39:
Chapter 40:
Chapter 41:
Chapter 42:
Chapter 43:
Chapter 44:
Prologue:
About the author:

Shattered

(Based on a true story)

By Valerie Bowen

Chapter 1

The smoke filled bar was loud for a Friday night. Bob Seger's Old Time Rock and Roll rattled the walls of the small tavern. Tanya was dancing in her chair when a stranger showed up. He stood on the opposite side of the table, beer in hand and his dark eyes were fixed on her. Feeling uncomfortable by his penetrating stare, she rose to her feet and walked to the bar.

Ray, the bartender, always had an eye for Tanya. She rested her arms on the bar, laced her fingers and waited for Ray to finish pouring a drink. After a few short moments, he approached her with a huge smile on his face. "Tanya, have you come for another drink? Or, have you come to ask me to take you home?" He winked.

"Oh Ray." She said with a smile on her face. "To tell you the truth, I had to get away from that guy." She jerked her head toward the table.

Ray glanced at the table where she had been sitting. "Do you mean the guy staring at you?"

She leaned across the bar and whispered. "Please tell me you're joking."

"It's no joke Tanya. That guy hasn't taken his eyes off you since he walked in."

"Ray, I need a shot…give me a tequila." She drummed her hands of the thick wood bar. "Damn it, I hate when men stare at me like that. It's so…aggravating."

He laughed. "Well, I have to admit he has good taste."

A guttural growl escaped her throat. "Come on Ray, I'm serious. That guy gives me the creeps."

He knitted his brows and stared into her eyes. "You're serious. Tanya, I won't let anything happen to you…ah, you do know that right?"

"Oh Ray, I don't think he'd hurt me. I just can't stand feeling like I'm the meat choice of the day." Bad experiences in her past, has caused Tanya to shy away from men, especially men who acted like they were choosing their next meal…or victim.

After placing the tequila on the bar in front of her, Ray leaned on the bar and put his face close to hers. "Don't worry about him, I think he's just interested…like I am."

Tanya straightened, lifted the tiny glass and tossed the pungent liquid back. She shuddered when the burn of the alcohol hit her throat. "Thanks, I needed that." She said as she placed the glass on the bar. "I'm going back to the table. I swear if that guy continues to gawk at me…"

Ray laughed out loud. "You'll do what? Call your favorite bartender over to handle the situation?"

Tanya raised a dark eyebrow. Her blue eyes sparkled when she twisted her head. "I'll…I'll…" She hung her head before turning. "You're right; I'll call you over to handle it."

Ray laughed out loud. "All I ask is, you take it easy on him. If I have to step in, I swear I'll pummel the guy's face. Just remember, I still need my job." He smiled as he wiped the bar with his small white towel. Tanya turned and walked away.

When Tanya returned to the table, her watcher was leaving. She watched the door close behind him from the corner of her eyes. She released a huge sigh. "Thank God that man's gone."

Pam, Tanya's best friend stared at her from her seated position. "What did you do to Gary?"

"What did I do?" She placed her seven and seven on the table and flopped down in her chair. "I didn't do anything."

"Oh…really." She smiled. "I think you did. I've known Gary Antonio for years. He's a player, I'll give him that, but he has never looked at a woman the way he looked at you."

Tanya's top lip curled up on one side. "Well, now that you told me…."

"Oh Tanya." Pam said with an evil grin on her face. "You could play with him, like he plays with every woman."

Tanya pinched the little plastic stirrer in her drink and moved it around. The jukebox was silent for a moment. Ice clinked on the side of the glass. She released a heavy sigh. "Pam I'm not playing with that guy. He's just too…too…"

"Weird." Pam said as she crossed her arms and leaned back in her chair. "That's the beauty of it. He'll think he's playing with you, but in reality, you're playing him."

Tanya lifted her drink, took a sip and returned it to the table. She shook her head. "No, I just wouldn't feel right. I know you said he was a player, but two wrongs don't make a right. Besides, the guy gives me the creeps."

Changing the subject, Pam said, "I noticed you were talking to Ray. What did he have to say?"

"The usual. He knew I was nervous, so he tried to ease the tension." Tanya stared into Pam's eyes. "He acts like…well, he acts like he likes me."

Pam burst out laughing. "Tanya you're so naive some times. Ray more than likes you. Every time I come in here he asks about you…that guy's crushing on you hard." She leaned forward. "You could have any man in here. Hell your dark hair and big blue eyes seem to drive the guys crazy."

Tanya blushed. "Come on Pam, I'm far from special." She scanned the room. "Look at all these women, there are so many that I'd consider gorgeous. I'm just average compared to her." She directed her friend's attention toward a tall thin blonde.

Pam clicked her tongue. "Tanya, you think of yourself as the bottom of the barrel. If I took a poll, from all the guys in here right now…you'd win hands down."

"Alright, enough of this praising the hell out of Tanya crap. How about, we leave here, and go to that new bar across town?"

Pam agreed. They rose to her feet and walked to the door. As Tanya passed the bar, she lifted her hand and gave Ray a shy smile. They stepped through the door and into the warm June evening.

Chapter 2

Two weeks later Pam invited Tanya to dinner. Pam's mom was a great cook and when she heard Mrs. Costa was making her special spaghetti and meatballs, she couldn't refuse. Tanya pulled in front of the small cape an hour later. After shifting to park and removing the key from the ignition, she climbed out. Leaning into the front seat, she grabbed her purse and the loaf of fresh Italian bread she had picked up on the way. She pushed the door closed with a jerk of her hip.

Walking up the driveway, Tanya didn't notice the pair of legs sticking out from under Mrs. Costa car before she tripped. She heard a muffled "Ouch." and the clanking of a metal tool hitting the pavement.

Embarrassed, Tanya looked down at the feet and apologized loudly. "Oh, sorry, I didn't see you." She turned and approached the door.

Pam opened the door as soon as she heard Tanya's apology. "Hey Tanya." She said loud enough for the entire neighborhood to hear. "I'm so glad you came. Mom's been cooking all morning." She swung the door open and stepped aside granting Tanya entry.

As she entered the kitchen, Tanya inhaled deeply, savoring the aroma of fresh tomato sauce. She noticed Mrs. Costa standing in front of the stove stirring a large pot of pasta. Steam wafted in the air around her. With wooden spoon in hand the woman turned to face the new comer. She gasped as if she hadn't seen Tanya in years. She placed the spoon on the counter and rushed to her with her arms outstretched. "There's my second daughter." Mrs. Costa pulled her into a tight embrace and kissed her firmly on the cheek. After releasing her she said, "I haven't seen you in a couple of weeks. What have you been doing with yourself?" She led Tanya to the table, pulled out a chair and gestured for her to sit.

Tanya smiled. She always felt so welcome when she came for a visit. Mrs. Costa always made her feel like one of the family. "Oh you know, working mostly. The shop's been very busy and there's mandatory overtime." She held the bakery bag up and Mrs. Costa smiled brightly. "I brought you your favorite bread." She handed the sack to the woman. "It's still warm."

Mrs. Costa grasped the bag, opened the top and inhaled. "You know you spoil me with this bread. I may have to ask you to come for dinner every night."

"Oh Mrs. Costa, you know I'd bring you bread every time I come over if I was sure you wanted it." She watched as the woman slid the bread from the bag and sliced it. Tanya knitted her brows. "Is there something wrong with your car?"

Pausing, Mrs. Costa turned to face her with a long blade knife in her hand. "No nothing's wrong. One of Pam's friends offered to do an oil change for me."

"That's nice. I wish someone would offer to change my oil. I also think I need a tune-up."

Pam stood in front of the stove listening to the conversation. "I know someone who'd give your car a tune-up." She shrugged as she pulled a strand of pasta from the pot and blew on it. "As a matter of fact I'll ask him as soon as he comes in...he's having dinner with us."

Tanya scowled. "Is this a set-up?"

Mrs. Costa chuckled as she placed the plate of bread on the table. "Why would you think that dear?"

"It's just..." Tanya paused for a brief moment. "Pam's always trying to set me up with guys. I'll have you know..." She glared at her best friend. "I don't need setting up. I'm doing perfectly fine on my own."

Mrs. Costa grasped the nape of Tanya's neck and firmly kissed the top of her head. "Don't get defensive, Pam isn't setting you up. I asked the young man if he wanted to stay for dinner. I thought it was the least I could do since he isn't charging me for the job."

"That's nice of you." She noticed Pam's body tense. "Pam, is there something wrong?

She held her gaze on the pot of pasta, and stammered. "Ah…no, I was…I…ah…"

Mrs. Costa grinned. "I think Pam likes the young man."

"No I don't." She snapped. "I just don't understand why you had to invite him today." *Of all days.* She thought as she hefted the pot with both hands and poured the contents into the waiting colander.

"Well I'm sure the guy will fall in love with your spaghetti and meatballs. Then, I'll have to fight him for a place at the table." Tanya said with certainty.

Just then the door swung open and Tanya's smile diminished. Gary said, without noticing the people in the room. "Your car's all set." He approached the hallway leading to the bathroom, and stopped dead in his tracks. "Hello Tanya." He said with a big toothy grin. "It's nice seeing you again."

Tanya scowled. She wondered how he knew her name. Then it donned on her, Pam's big mouth told him. "Hello." She said meekly.

Mrs. Costa looked from Gary to Tanya then back again. "You two know each other?"

Tanya immediately spoke up. "We never really met, I saw him in the bar a couple of weeks ago." Her eyes shifted to Pam and Tanya gritted her teeth.

"Gary, go clean up in the bathroom. Dinner will be on the table in a minute."

He obeyed but not before he gave Tanya a stare full of lust. He softly smiled and brushed past her chair.

Tanya cringed when she felt the heat of his body. Once she was positive he was in the bathroom, she whispered loudly. "Why didn't you tell me he was here? I have a good mind to leave."

Mrs. Costa was surprised. "Sweetheart, if I knew he had this effect on you, I would've made him dinner another night. Please don't blame Pam…it's my fault for inviting him."

Pam placed a large bowl of pasta and sauce on the table. She looked into Tanya's eyes and gave her an apologetic smile. She mouthed. "Sorry." She bared her teeth and returned to her task.

By the time Gary returned to the table Tanya had calmed. She knew Mrs. Costa wasn't aware of the bar incident and how Gary had made her feel. She enjoyed the meal knowing after dinner she wouldn't have to see him again unless their paths crossed again. They exchanged pleasantries and Tanya thought he was nice enough, but not her type.

Chapter 3

In a small park, on Independence Day, Tanya sat in a lawn chair enjoying a conversation with a few friends. The aroma of hamburgers and hotdogs floated through the air. A slight breeze lifted a lock of her hair and she swept it behind her ear. She looked up when she heard a woman calling her name. "Hey Tanya, I want you to meet somebody."

Turning to face the woman, she realized the voice came from an old high school friend. Tanya's mouth gaped when she noticed who she was dragging along. "Hey Lori, how are you doing?" Tanya eyed the man standing beside her.

"I'm doing great. I want you to meet someone."

Tanya murmured, "We've already met."

Lori raised an eye brow. "You have?" She turned to the man. "Gary, you said you wanted to get to know Tanya."

He smiled brightly. "I do. I've only been able to talk to her once and I'd really like to get to know her better."

Tanya turned to face Pam. "Did you put him up to this?"

She shook her head. "I introduced him to Lori a couple of weeks ago. Believe me; I didn't know he would play her, like he tried to play me."

Gary crouched down beside Tanya and placed his hands on the armrest of her chair. "Can't you at least give me the time of day?"

She scowled down at his hands, and then looked into his dark brown eyes. "Truthfully, I have enough on my plate right now."

"Well, won't you at least give me your phone number?"

She wondered if the guy had rocks for brains. "I don't think so. I think I already said I had enough on my plate."

He furrowed his brow. "I guess if you won't give your number to me, I'll have to find a way to get it." He straightened, and approached Lori. "You'll give it to me…won't you?"

Lori looked at Tanya who was shaking her head. "I don't know." She said hesitantly. "I wouldn't want Tanya to get mad at me."

Tanya knew men like Gary Antonio, couldn't be deterred. She watched as he shrugged his shoulders, turned and walked away with Lori following close behind.

Tanya looked into Pam's eyes. "What the hell is wrong with that guy? It's like he doesn't know the meaning of the word no."

Pam tried to sound logical when she said, "Well it's not like you actually told him no."

"Yes I did!"

"Actually you said you had enough on your plate right now…I think he took it as, you'd possibly give him your number in the future."

Tanya blew out a huge sigh. "Why is it, men don't think the way women do? I mean, it would be so much easier if we were all on the same page…don't you agree?"

Pam giggled. "I don't think that'll happen in our life time. Men are far from logical thinkers."

As the sun dipped behind the mountain, an orange and purple hue washed over the sky. The two girls called it a day, packed their gear in the trunk of Pam's car, and headed home.

On the way Pam said enthusiastically, "Why don't we go to Larry's?" Her tone turned devilish. "I'm sure Ray's working tonight."

Tanya was digging through her purse. After a brief moment she pulled out a package of gum, removed two sticks and handed one to Pam. "I don't know." Tanya sighed as she chewed. "I don't really want to run into Gary again. You know, he's always around lately…I wonder why."

Pam lifted her brows. "Are you kidding me? That guy has his eyes on you…you're like the only woman that hasn't fallen head over heels for him. You have to admit the guy talks a good talk."

Tanya bit the corner of her lips. "Oh…that he does." She placed her purse on the floorboard. "I know! Why don't we go see a movie? I'm sure there's something good playing."

Pam thought for a brief moment. "Oh…I know, we can get drunk and go bowling!"

Tanya burst out laughing. "I guess if I'm going to have to embarrass myself bowling, I might as well do it drunk."

"Great, let's go to my house and call a few people and we'll do this." Pam slammed her hand down on the steering wheel and started laughing. "Remember the last time we did this?" Tanya scowled. "Remember you tripped over the ball return and your ball flew two lanes away…if I recall you knocked four pins down." Pam roared, tears flooded her eyes as the memory played out in her mind. She had to pull to the side of the road until she regained her composure.

Tanya started to giggle. "Yeah the guy, whose lane it was, seemed shocked when my ball came flying out of nowhere into his lane." She laughed so hard her sides began to hurt. "Oh my God…his face…it was definitely a Kodak moment." Tanya wrapped her arms around her abdomen. "Oh, stop…I can't take it any more…"

A tapping sound came on the driver's window and caused Pam to jump. She glanced up and then back at Tanya while she tried, unsuccessfully, to halt the laughter. As she cranked down the window, an officer leaned in. He shined his flashlight into the car and smiled as soon as he realized nothing was wrong. "Do you girls need assistance?" He said while eyeing the two giggling girls.

Pam tried to calm her laughter enough to explain. "We're fine. Sorry, I had to pull over because…" She calmed, ran her hand through her shoulder length blonde hair and stared up at the smiling officer. "Sorry about that. I had to pull over because she had me laughing so hard I couldn't see to drive." She jabbed a thumb in Tanya's direction.

The officer was a muscular man with short dark hair. His green eyes twinkled in the moon light. "I don't know why you were laughing, but it had to be damned good judging by the looks of things." He flipped the switch and his flashlight went dark. Before he straightened his back he said, "Since you girls are alright…take your time to relax and…ah have a nice night."

Pam cranked up the window, turned on her blinker, and pulled onto the road. She tried to hold back her laughter with little success. "Could you imagine having to call our parents to bail us out of jail?" Her voice deepened. "Hello, Mrs. Costa, I'm afraid you're going to have to come to the police station to bail your daughter out."

Tanya played along. She said in falsetto. "I don't understand…why was she arrested?"

Pam with her deep voice replied. "I'm afraid she was laughing…"

The two girls roared.

Chapter 4

With the mandatory overtime at work, Tanya barely had energy enough to go home, eat dinner and climb into bed. Working twelve hours a day in an electronics factory was slowly killing her social life. Two weeks passed and Tanya has not only managed to keep a distance between her and Gary, but was far too drained to go out with her friends. Climbing into bed, Tanya glanced at the clock and yawned. She thought, *thankfully tomorrow's Saturday...there's no more overtime, so I can sleep in.*

She was startled awake by the ringing of her phone. Her eyes were full of sleep when she glanced at the clock, and realized it was twelve fifteen. As she fumbled for the phone in the darkness, she wondered who in their right mind would call a person so late. Lifting the receiver from the cradle, she mumbled, "Hello?"

"Tanya...how are you?"

Her eyes lost their sleepiness and she bolted up into a sitting position. Anger flooded her body. "Gary? Where...how did you get my number?"

"Lori gave it to me." If it had been possible, steam would've erupted from her ears. She gritted her teeth and listened. "I'm calling to ask if you'll go out with me."

"Gary, I'm not going to discuss this right now. Please call me back at a decent hour." She started to remove the phone from her ear.

"Wait, please don't hang up! I just want to know, if you'll at least consider dating me…that's all. Just please promise me, you'll at least think about it."

Tanya blew out a puff of air. "Gary, I'm sure this is important to you but…"

He interrupted her. "You don't understand…" Panic was in his tone.

Tanya gave up and flopped back onto her pillow. She knew by the way he was talking; it would be a while before she could get a word in. She closed her eyes and listened to the sound of his deep voice. She was startled awake by the awful tone the phone company sent across the line alerting her the phone was off the hook. Her ear throbbed; she rubbed the tender appendage and returned the receiver to the cradle. "Damn." She said out loud, "I can't believe I fell asleep on the phone." She glanced at the clock on her bedside table. *Two thirty*…she thought, *he must've talked all that time without knowing I was asleep.* Giggling she returned to her comfortable position and fell back asleep.

By the time Tanya awoke, it was nine thirty. Although she didn't feel well rested, she was happy she didn't have to work.

Preparing for her day, she took a shower and immediately dressed. Determined to make every minute count, she lifted the receiver and started dialing Pam's number. Tanya paused before she tapped the final button. She remembered her friend had already made plans for the day. She returned the receiver to the cradle and was surprised when the phone immediately started ringing. "Hello?"

Lori was on the line and clearly upset. "Oh Tanya...I did something I'm sure you'll hate me for."

She raked her fingers through her damp hair. She knew her friend was calling to apologize. "If you're calling to tell me you gave that guy Gary my number, you don't have to...he called me late last night."

"Honestly Tanya, I don't know why I gave it to him. I knew if you wanted him to have it you would've given it to him...but the man is relentless. He called me day and night for two solid weeks begging. Finally I couldn't take it anymore so I...I"

Tanya knew her friend was nearly in tears when she explained the situation. Understanding, she softly said, "Don't worry about it. I just think the guy's lonely. He called me last night and no lie...he carried on a conversation all by himself. I figure he talked for two hours." Tanya giggled. "I fell asleep and woke to the stupid tone the phone company sends when the receiver's off the hook…you know the one, beep, beep, beep…it's so annoying you have no choice but to pay attention to it. Besides, I think he must've got the hint when I didn't talk back. I don't think he'll be calling back."

"I don't know, he seems like he's very interested in you. He always asks about you. As a matter of fact, now that I think about it, you're the topic of all our conversations."

Tanya plucked a piece of lint from her comforter and rolled it between her forefinger and thumb. Sitting cross-legged on her bed, she sighed. "Lori, can you do me a favor? If he mentions my name again, just tell him you don't feel comfortable talking about me. That should stop him from harassing you."

"I'll do it, but I don't think he'll stop…the guy is obsessed."

"I have a few things I have to get done this afternoon. Why don't you meet Pam and me at Larry's later tonight? We'll take in a movie or something. I just don't want to hang around there. I'd rather not see that guy on my first night out in two weeks."

"Oh we can hang out there. Gary works nights at some machine shop."

Tanya's eyes lit up. "Great, then we can have a few drinks while we decide what we're going to do."

Tanya ended the call feeling satisfied knowing she could go out and have a good time without worrying about Gary showing up.

Pam wanted to go to a new bar where a popular local band was playing. By the time Tanya convinced Pam to leave the noisy bar, her head was pounding and all she could think about was her bed. Tanya entered her house a little after midnight. Climbing the stairs to her room, she was happy to have few minutes to read before she turned off her light. Just as she finished getting ready for bed, her phone rang. She stared at the menacing device and then glanced at the clock. She sat down on her bed, sighed and picked up the receiver. "Hello?" She knew who her late night caller was before he uttered a word.

"Hey Tanya. I'm calling to ask if you'd like to meet me for a drink."

"Gary I just got home." She released an audible sigh. "My head is throbbing, my ears hurt and all I want to do is sleep."

"Oh." Disappointment was in his tone. "Maybe we can just talk."

"I guess you can talk for a little while, but I'm not promising I won't fall asleep…again."

"That's great…."

He continued his rambling while Tanya rose to her feet, pulled back the covers and climbed into bed. After releasing a heavy yawn she interrupted his spiel. "I really have to go. I don't think I can keep my eyes open."

It was as if she hadn't said a word. The man kept talking. Finally giving up, Tanya laid her head on the pillow and fell asleep. She was startled awake by the beep, beep, beep, sound when it entered her ear. She removed the receiver from her ear and placed it in the cradle. *I have no idea what that man talks about, but he definitely can put me to sleep.* She thought as she returned to her comfortable position.

Two weeks passed and the phone calls persisted. Every night like clockwork Tanya's phone rang at twelve fifteen and Gary would be on the other end. Fed up with the evening intrusions she finally decided she had to put an end to it.

Tanya sat on the edge of her bed staring at the narrow princess phone. The cord connecting the receiver to the base was twisted and distorted from years of fidgeting with it while she talked. The phone rang. "Hello." She said after picking it up on the first ring.

"Hey Tanya, it's…"

"I know who it is. I don't know anyone else who would call a person every night after midnight."

"I just called to ask if you'd like to go out for something to eat."

Tanya hung her head. She couldn't believe, after two weeks of trying to get rid of the man, he was still determined to go out on a date with her. She stared down at the floor.

The wind outside pelted her window with tiny bits of sand and debris. "Gary, I've told you numerous times, I don't want to date you."

"I know, but I'm hoping if I continue to ask, you'll change your mind." He sighed into the phone. His voice was soft when he said, "Please. All I'm asking for is a chance to get to know you."

Fed up and tired, Tanya clenched her teeth. "Alright. I'll go on one date with you."

"Great I'll be right over."

"Wait a minute." She said with panic in her tone. "I didn't mean I'd go out with you tonight."

Gary sounded excited. "When? Name the day and the time and I'll be there."

"Next Saturday, eight o'clock." She paused. "If you're not here at eight, I'm leaving."

"I swear I'll be there." Gary hung up without saying another word. *Wow that was easy,* she thought as she returned the handset to the cradle. *Now I need to come up with a plan…if he's not here at eight, I will leave.* Tuning down the covers, Tanya climbed into bed knowing she wouldn't be disturbed.

Chapter 5

By the time Saturday rolled around, Tanya had devised a well thought out plan. As the hours ticked away slowly, Tanya was determined to get out of the date with Gary. She called Pam and Lori and asked them to park in the lot close to her parents. Then when he didn't show up at eight, she'd leave the house and him in the dust.

It was six thirty when Tanya dialed Pam's number to make final arrangements. "...so you're absolutely positive you'll be in the parking lot."

"Geez Tanya, I've been telling you all week, we'll be there. You have to calm down."

She paced the kitchen stretching the phone cord to the limit. "I know, I know. It's just...well, I only agreed to this date to get him off the phone." She sighed. "I didn't want to agree. I just couldn't figure out any other way to make him stop calling me in the middle of the night."

Pam's voice was comforting. "Sweetie, when you see him tonight..."

"What do you mean when? How do you know he's not going to be late?"

"I know you'll see him, because he's been bragging about your date to everyone we know. Trust me; he's planning on being at your house by seven forty-five, just to make sure he's on time. He said he wasn't taking any chances on missing the date he worked so hard to get."

"Well that's just great!" The long phone cord bounced when she jerked her arm. "Why is he so determined?"

"Tanya, you can take it one of two ways. First, he's going through all this trouble because he really likes you, or he refuses to be turned down. You know I'd swear it's the first scenario. He does nothing but talk about you all the time."

Tanya twisted her finger in the coils of the cord. "Now what? I don't have a good feeling about this guy...there's something in my gut telling me to run."

"Oh please, now you're sounding like that psychic I went to visit last week. I think he's harmless."

"You went to a psychic? Why?"

Pam laughed. "I thought the woman could tell me if and when I'd find mister right. All she told me was my karma is dark and she wanted me to pay her a hundred and fifty bucks to clean it. I really don't think you can clean someone's karma. Anyway, back to Gary. Lori and I will be in the parking lot as planned. If you don't show up by eight fifteen, we're leaving."

"Sounds fair." Tanya untwisted the wire she had been fidgeting with and stepped to the wall where the cradle hung. "Let me go so I can finish getting ready for the…ah, date. I'll talk to you later."

The phone hung on the wall next to a tall window overlooking the yard. She glanced through the glass, and noticed a blue jay was perched on a low tree branch eyeing a little grey squirrel. All of a sudden the bird dove toward the squirrel sending the terrified animal scurrying toward the safety of a nearby bush. Tanya laughed. *Better watch it, if you're the same bird that's been aggravating Rufus…*Tanya's thoughts were interrupted when her mother, Sherry, entered the room.

"Tanya, what has you so deep in thought?"

"Oh nothing mom. I was just watching a blue jay terrorize a squirrel."

"That bird better mind his business; I know Rufus has just about had enough of him. Do you know, he attacks that cat when he sits on the porch railing? That animal will get that bird…mark my words." Sherry sat in her favorite chair and stared up into Tanya's eyes. "Are you and Pam going out tonight?"

Tanya turned to face her mother. "No." She said while releasing a heavy breath. "I have a date." After pulling out the chair across from her mother, she slumped down into the seat.

Sherry smiled. "Oh, do I know the young man?"

She shook her head. "No, and hopefully I won't know him for much longer."

"Why do you say that? If you don't…"

"It's a long story and I really don't feel like discussing Gary right now."

Sherry watched Tanya pull a paper napkin from the holder and started tearing it apart. "Why did you agree to date him? I mean, you're far from excited. I would…"

Tanya rose to her feet and stepped toward the stairs. "Mom, I really don't feel like discussing this right now. Besides, I have to finish getting ready. I'll talk to you later."

A knock sounded on the front door as Tanya was descending the stairs. "I'll get it." She said while walking to the door. She glanced at the clock on the wall and cringed. *Wouldn't you know seven fifty-nine…well, let's get this date out of the way so I can get on with my life.*

Tanya sucked in a deep breath and released it slowly while turning the knob. After swinging the door open, she said, "Hi Gary, how are you tonight?"

Gary had a broad grin on his face when he looked at her pretty face. It took a moment for him to respond. "Wow Tanya, you look great."

She wore a pair of blue jeans and white blouse. Her long dark hair displayed decorative combs placed just above her ears.

Her natural waves cascaded down her back. "Thanks Gary." She said as she stepped through the door and onto the porch.

"I thought we could get a bite to eat then maybe we could take in a movie."

Tanya shrugged. "Sounds good." He wrapped an arm around her waist. She tensed when she felt the heat of his arm radiate through the thin fabric of her blouse.

Gary rushed to the car, pulled open the passenger door, and waited until she was safely inside. Tanya's brows knitted. *Wow, I don't think I've ever had a man open a car door for me.* She watched as he rounded the car. She finally noticed his outfit. He wore a pair of white dress pants and a matching vest. She wanted to laugh but didn't have the heart. *Why the hell would he wear white to go to a movie…he's so dressed up…*

Gary slid into the car, reached into the backseat and pulled out a huge bouquet of red roses. "I thought you might like these."

Tanya was speechless when she grasped the hefty gift. She held two dozed deep red roses decorated with white baby's breath and dark green ferns. She pressed her nose to one of blossom and inhaled. If he was trying to work his way into her heart, he was doing a fine job. "These are beautiful…you really sho…"

Gary interrupted. "Shhh, I thought you'd like them." He smiled as he twisted the key and the engine came to life. "I was thinking, we could go to that new Chinese place in town…" He gasped. "I'm sorry, I didn't even ask, do you like Chinese?"

Tanya noticed his tension. "I love Chinese. I rarely have it; most of my friends prefer pizza or burgers."

"Great, I'm glad I made a good decision."

Gary and Tanya had a great meal. They shared a pu-pu platter and lo-mien. He was slowly easing his way into her good graces. Proving to be the perfect gentleman in every way, he reached for her hand, and stared into her eyes. "Would you like to go to a movie, or would you prefer to go to Larry's to see your friends?"

Tanya was excited he actually asked for her opinion. She smiled shyly. "If you don't mind, I'd like to go the Larry's."

"Sounds great to me. I just love spending time with you."

By the time Gary delivered her home, Tanya's feelings for him had changed. She realized he wasn't as bad as she initially thought. He walked her to her front door and said softly, "I hope we can do this again sometime. I had a great night."

She pulled her key from her purse, turned her back to him and paused before she slid it into the lock. She felt Gary's hand on her shoulder. His warm breath brushed past her ear. "May I kiss you good night?"

Turning to face him, she bit her lip and nodded. He wrapped his arms around her, and touched his lips to hers. The kiss was sweet and tender. "Thanks for the great evening." He said after releasing her. He gently swept a stray lock of hair behind her ear while staring into her eyes He kissed her once more, and waited for her to enter the house before turning to leave.

Chapter 6

It had been two months since Gary and Tanya's first date. For her the relationship was more to keep the phone calls at a minimum than anything else. Every time they went out, he treated her like a queen. There was something about him that just didn't sit right with her. The only way she could explain it, he was either fake or trying too hard. Either way, she couldn't picture herself in a long term relationship with him.

While sitting at the table having coffee with her mother, Tanya heard a knock on the door. She rose to her feet, approached the door and smiled when she recognized the visitor. She swung the door open and greeted her mother's friend. "Hello Millie, I haven't seen you in ages. How have you been?"

The woman stepped across the threshold and walked toward the kitchen. "I'm good, how have you been?" She stood beside the table, scanned Tanya from head to toe and scowled. "Why didn't you tell me you were pregnant?"

All the color drained from Tanya's face. She stammered. "Wha...what? I'm not..." She grasped the back of one of the heavy oak chairs and tried to catch her breath. "I can't…Oh God…"

Millie looked at Sherry and said with certainty. "She is pregnant."

Sherry didn't know what to say. She watched as Tanya pulled the chair away from the table and flopped into it. She folded her arms on the table and buried her face. Sherry knew Tanya was just as stunned as she was. "Millie how do you know? I don't think Tanya even knew."

Millie shrugged. "I have always been able to tell when a woman's pregnant."

"Tanya, sweetheart. I'm going to the store to pick up one of those early pregnancy tests. You need to know for sure if you're pregnant or not, before you go out and do something stupid."

Tanya sobbed. Sherry strained to understand her muffled words. "Mom, what the hell am I going to do? I can't be…Oh God I'm only twenty-one."

Sherry rose to her feet and approached Tanya's chair. She lovingly rubbed her daughter's back. "Don't worry sweetheart. You don't have to think about anything until you get the results." Sherry turned to face Millie. "Would you mind staying here with Tanya while I go get the pregnancy test?"

"Why don't you let me go? Besides, I think Tanya needs her mother right now."

Sherry agreed. "Tanya while Millie's gone, I want you to go lay down on the sofa. You have to calm down, and you won't be able to do that in a chair. I don't want you to start thinking you're pregnant if you actually aren't."

After a few long moments, Tanya rose to her feet and dried her eyes on a paper napkin. "You're right. There's no reason for me to worry. What could be the worst thing that could happen? If I'm pregnant I'm pregnant." She shrugged one shoulder. Tanya was determined not to allow the possible pregnancy to consume her rational thinking. She stared out the window; her voice was calm and soft. "No matter what, I'll have to deal with the consequences of my actions. If I am, I refuse to have an abortion…if I'm not; I'll have to go to the doctor to get a prescription for 'the pill'. I'm not going to let an unplanned pregnancy change my life."

"Tanya, you tried those pills…you can't take them! The doctor took you off those things couple of years ago…you had blood clots in your legs…you can't take them!" Sherry started to panic. "We'll figure out something, let's just take this slow." Sherry calmed. "Day by day, we'll take it step by step, we'll get you through this."

Millie returned with the home pregnancy test. After handing the small carton to Shelly, she proceeded to pour a cup of coffee. "I read the instructions while I waited in line to pay. It says you'll have the results in just a few hours. Imagine, a test you can do at home and you can get results quicker than if you took it in the doctor's office. Technology has come a long way in the past decade. I can remember having to wait a week or more before the doctor gave me the news." She pulled out a chair and sat. "There's one thing you have to keep in mind Tanya. You can always come to me if you have questions or need anything."

Tanya removed the box from her mother's hand and stepped into the bathroom. Before closing the door she turned to face the two older women. "Who knows, this could be a blessing in disguise." She closed the door and proceeded to take the test.

It took four hours for the test to reveal the answer. As the time drew closer, Tanya nervously bit her fingernails. Staring up at the clock, Tanya's stomach tensed. "I guess it's time." She rose to her feet and entered the bathroom. The small plastic box stood on the vanity among the decorative soap dish and toothbrush holder. Tanya stared down at the narrow test tube suspended above a small mirror secured to the bottom of the container. Holding the instructions from the kit in her hand, she glanced from the image on the paper to the mirror in the container and her eyes welled with tears. *Positive*. She thought as she placed the paper beside the plastic cube. *Now what the hell am I going to do? How am I supposed to tell Gary? I can't believe I was so irresponsible.*

A stray tear rolled down her face and she swept it away with the back of her hand. As she approached the closed door Tanya could hear her mother talking to her father in the living room. Unable to make out the hushed mummers, she opened the door and approached them. The knot in her stomach tensed with each step she took. Standing in the center of the room, her head bowed and her hands fidgeted, Tanya said, "Millie was right. The test is positive."

"Oh baby." Her father approached her with his arms spread wide. "Come here." Tanya stepped forward and was immediately wrapped in his loving embrace. He kissed the side of her head while her tears dampened the shoulder of his shirt. "Everything's going to be fine. Your mother and I will do everything we can to help you take care of the little tyke."

Tanya eased out of her father's embrace and dried her tear stained face with the back of her hands. "Oh daddy, I don't know what I'm going to do."

Sherry spoke up. "I know what you're going to do…you're going to tell the father and he'll have to help you."

"Sherry!" Her husband snapped. "We have to let Tanya figure out what she's going to do." He turned his eyes and stared into Tanya's. "I want you to relax and take this slow. There's no need to drag the man into this just yet. Figure out how you'll tell him before you approach him…" Tanya hung her head. "Look at me." She returned her eyes to his. "I don't want you to think for one minute you are alone. I'm here, and your mother's here. We can do this."

Tanya bit her lip and continued to fidget. "I know that. I just don't want Gary to think he has to marry me. To be completely honest, I don't want to marry him."

"If he asks you, you have to marry him." Sherry said in an authority in her tone. "It's the right thing to do…for the baby."

Tanya had always suffered at the hands of bullies and her mother had been very strict. That combination of abuse caused Tanya to shy away from any altercation. Tanya had a problem with confrontation as well as voicing her opinion. She knew she would do exactly as her mother told her. Yes she was an adult and yes she was the one that had to live with her decisions no matter how they were made. She still felt it was easier to please her mother than to suffer her wrath.

Chapter 7

Later that evening Tanya was lying in bed with her arms crossed behind her head. Her eyes were red and puffy, although the tears had stopped flowing hours ago. She waited in the darkness for the twelve fifteen phone call she had grown accustomed to receiving. In the two months Gary and Tanya had been dating, he hadn't missed a night. At twelve ten Tanya sat up and clicked on the bedside lamp. The knot in her stomach hadn't eased. As the minutes grew closer to the dreaded phone call, the knot grew tighter. She sat on her hands trying to stop them from trembling.

Just like clockwork the ringing phone disturbed the silence of the home. By the time the second ring entered the room Tanya lifted her hand and placed it on the receiver. Her hand trembled and her fingers seemed to have a mind of their own. She nervously chewed on her bottom lip and lifted the receiver after the third ring. Her voice shuddered when she spoke. "Hello?"

Gary sounded concerned. "Tanya, what's wrong?"

She twisted the cord around her finger. "Oh…ah, nothing. I just had a very trying day."

"Trying, in what way? Do you need me to come over?"

Tanya lifted the cradle from the bedside table, walked to the opposite side of the room, placed the base on the dresser and stared at her reflection in her mirror. Tears welled in her eyes. She choked back her sobs. "If you don't mind Gary, can we talk later?"

"No Tanya, I need to know what's going on with you. Why do you sound so upset?"

"I'm not." She lied. "I'm just really tired and I think I should go to bed.

Gary's tone deepened. "Tanya I know something's bothering you. I won't be able to sleep unless I know you're alright." He sucked in a breath and released it. "I'll be there in fifteen minutes. I'm going to need you to meet me outside; I don't want to ring the bell and wake your parents. We can go for a drink or…"

"Gary you don't have to…"

"Yes I do, now promise me you'll meet me outside."

Tears trickled from her eyes. "Alright, I'll meet you." She didn't wait for him to say his usual goodnight; she stared in the mirror and automaton like, she returned the receiver to the base.

Gary drove into the driveway less than fifteen minutes later. He leapt from the car and rushed to Tanya's side. He wrapped her in his arms, kissed the top of her head and whispered, "Tanya, your trembling." He eased her away and stared into her eyes. "Tanya…" his eyes tried to remain in a fixed position, but he found himself scanning her face. "Babe, what's wrong?"

She tried to hold back her tears, but seeing his face opened the flood gates in her eyes. "Oh Gary, I don't know how you tell you this."

He scowled. "Are you breaking up with me?"

She shook her head. "No, maybe we should sit in the car. I'm getting a little chilly."

Gary wrapped an arm around her waist and quickly escorted her to his car. Once they were settled, Gary twisted in his seat so he could face her. "Tell me, what has you so upset." He handed her a paper napkin.

She removed the napkin from his hands and dried her eyes. Staring down and fidgeting with her fingers she said, "Gary, I'm…ah…pregnant." She looked into his eyes. "The reason I'm telling you…well I just thought you'd want to know…"

He interrupted. "So what's the plan?"

Tanya pursed her lips and scanned his face. "The plan is to have this baby and go on with my life. I don't expect anything from you, this is my problem."

"That's where you're wrong. It's not your problem it's our problem." He grasped both her hands and placed a tender kiss on each one. "There's no doubt in my mind what we have to do…" she stared into his eyes. "We'll get married…before the baby comes. We can do this before Christmas."

He beamed with excitement and she tensed. "Gary, I really don't think that's a good idea. Getting married because of a pregnancy never works out.

"I won't accept no for an answer." He placed a firm kiss on her soft lips. "I have to go. I have to make plans…damn; I'm going to be a husband and a father. I can't believe how lucky I am."

Tanya reached for the door release and pushed it open. She didn't know what to think about his reaction. She honestly couldn't believe he actually seemed happy. "Okay Gary, I'll see you sometime next week."

He quickly climbed out of the car and rushed to her side. "Oh no, I'll be seeing you every day. There's no way in hell I can ever go a day without seeing you" He beamed. "I am going to be your husband…I'm marrying the woman of my dreams."

Tanya was taken aback. "Hold on, I don't think this has sunk in yet. Go home get some rest and then if you still feel the same way in the morning, give me a call. I don't want to discuss marriage or babies or anything. I've had a very rough day. Right now all I want to do is get some sleep."

He gave her a passionate kiss, opened the front door and waited for her to step though, close and lock it. Returning to his car, he had a smile on his face and love in his heart.

Tanya walked into the house and to the kitchen. She halted in her tracks when she spied someone lurking in the darkness. Her heart began to race. Her voice was shaky when she stammered, "Who…who's there?"

Sherry's calming voice came out of the darkness. "It's me sweetheart."

Tanya flipped on the light. Her brows knitted. "What are you doing standing in the dark?"

"I heard Gary drive up…I was worried about you."

Tanya smiled. "Why would you worry about Gary? It's not like he'd do anything. As a matter of fact he's one of the sweetest guys I know."

Sherry turned toward the cabinets, opened one and pulled out two glasses. "Sweetie, grab the juice and have a seat. I want to talk to you."

Reaching into the refrigerator she pulled out the juice and pushed the door closed with a slight tap of her elbow. "Is there something wrong mom?"

"Did you tell Gary?"

"Yes mom. "She said with a huff. "Before you ask, he took the news very well.

As a matter of fact I think he was kind of happy."

Sherry placed the glasses on the table and Tanya removed the lid from the bottle and poured the cool liquid into the glasses. "Did he say what he thought you should do?"

While replacing the top on the bottle and returning it to the refrigerator, Tanya said, "As a matter of fact…" She eyed her mother's expression. "He wants to get married."

"That's good dear." Sherry smiled brightly. "At least he's taking responsibility."

"I don't want to marry him. I can raise this child on my own."

Sherry was in the process of taking a sip of her juice. After hearing Tanya's words, she removed the glass from her lips and scowled. "If he wants to marry you, you have to do it."

"I really don't think getting married because I'm pregnant is a great idea."

"Nonsense. He asked you, he wants to take responsibility you're going to marry him…it's the right thing to do."

"But mom, I don't want to get married."

"The man asked you to marry him, you're carrying his child…you will marry him."

Tanya hung her head. Her eyes welled with tears and she turned to leave the room. "Why don't I have a say in this? Why do I have to do something I'm not comfortable with?"

"This is all new to you. Believe me; once this all settles in, you'll see things differently."

"I doubt it." she murmured as she walked out of the room and climbed the stairs.

Chapter 8

The next two months passed quickly. Sherry kept talking about the wedding and all the things Tanya had to do to prepare. She was standing on front of the counter scooping grinds into the coffee makers basket. "You must be getting so excited. Just think tomorrow my baby will be married."

Tanya's stress level was mounting. Each passing day felt more like she was to going to her death, not her wedding. She was tired of her mother's constant harping. The only reason Tanya was getting married was because her mother continually told her 'it was the right thing to do'. Sherry was relentless with her badgering. Finally fed up Tanya growled. "Mom I don't want to discuss the stupid wedding, day in and day out. I'd pref…"

Sherry was reaching into the cabinet for cups. She spun around and glared at Tanya. The piercing look and her tone caused Tanya to clamp her mouth shut. "Of course we have to discuss it; you're getting married tomorrow. There are things you need to do."

More than a little perturbed, Tanya scraped up some courage and glared into her mother's eyes. "There's nothing to do! I'm getting married by the J.P., the blood tests have been done and Gary informed me last night he picked up the rings. So if you don't mind I'd like to be able to sit down and drink my coffee in peace." Tears trickled down her face. "I just don't want to think about this...this so called wedding."

"Watch your tone when you talk to me young lady. You're still my daughter and you still have to respect me." The coffee pot was at the end of the brew cycle. Steam and a loud gurgling sound erupted from the maker. After pouring two cups of coffee, Sherry returned the pot to the base, and carried the cups to the table. She placed one in front of Tanya and the other in front of her chair. She sat. "I don't know why you're so upset. Gary's a nice young man; he loves you and wants to take care of you...what more could a woman ask for?"

Sherry put the fear of God in Tanya when she was growing up; she also refused to allow Tanya to voice her opinion. In Sherry's eyes she was the mother and Tanya was the child...the child had to obey the mother or there were consequences. Pulling her eyes from Sherry's, Tanya prepared her coffee. "I'm sorry; I didn't mean to disrespect you. I guess I'm just nervous."

Sherry scoffed. "Oh sweetie, it's alright to be nervous." She said in a sickening sweet tone. "Every woman gets nervous. When your father and I were getting married, I worried about him getting cold feet and leaving me at the altar."

Tanya stirred her coffee as if she was mixing a cake. The hot beverage slopped over the sides and onto the clean tablecloth. "Damn it!" She glanced up and noticed her mother's scowling face. "Sorry mom, I'll clean it and put it into the washer.

"You sit and relax. I'll take care of it as soon as we're done. Knowing you, every cloth I own will have a stain on it by the time you finish your coffee."

Tanya tapped the spoon on the side of the cup and placed it on a folded paper napkin. Tears welled in her eyes. "How do women do it?"

"Do what dear."

"Marry a man they're not in love with."

Sherry glared at her daughter. "You loved him enough to get yourself in a bind. You made your bed, so you have to live with it."

A stray tear trickled down Tanya's cheek. "We had sex...you don't have to be in love...just horny."

"Tanya! You know I don't like hearing you talk like that." Sherry rose to her feet, grabbed the coffee carafe and poured another cup. Her tone calmed. "Don't worry, I'm sure over time you'll grow to love him. Right now all you have to do is get through tomorrow."

Tanya finished her coffee, placed her cup in the dishwasher and turned to face her mother. "I'm going upstairs to lie down. I haven't been feeling great lately…I think it has something to do with my nerves."

"You could be having morning sickness. I've heard some women have morning sickness throughout their entire pregnancy."

"It's not morning sickness…it's I'm getting married sickness." Tanya walked to the stairs. "I'll be down in a little while. Gary mentioned he was coming over later this afternoon."

"Doesn't he know it's bad luck to see the bride before the wedding?"

"Mom, does it really matter. It's not like a real wedding. Besides I can't see this situation getting much worse." Tanya climbed the stairs and flopped down face first on her bed and cried.

Chapter 9

It was seven o'clock the next morning when Tanya dragged herself out of bed. She padded off to the bathroom and stared at her reflection in the mirror. She was horrified by what she saw. If it hadn't been for her red puffy eyes, her face would have no color. She leaned in to get a closer look. *I look worse than I did when I spent the week in the hospital with the viral infection.* She straightened her back and prepared to take a shower.

Tanya dressed in a cream colored dress with gathers at the shoulders and waist. She stood in front of her full length mirror and scowled. *What the hell am I doing? How can I go through with this?* She thought. *I feel like a mail order bride with no choice. Yeah I had unprotected sex, but do I really have to marry the guy? I know so many single mothers that are doing just fine on their own…Maybe I should move to a different state."* A smile crossed her pretty face then she frowned. *My luck Gary and my mother would hunt me down and drag me back here.* She sighed and continued getting dressed.

It was nine fifteen when Tanya finally departed her room. She was expecting to see her mother standing in the kitchen with a shotgun in her hand to make certain she went through with the marriage fiasco. Upon entering the kitchen, Tanya was surprised her mother was nowhere to be seen. Tanya growled. "She didn't…she wouldn't go to the J.P.'s office…would she?" As she scanned the room Tanya noticed a sheet of paper lying on the table. With trembling hands she lifted the note and read:

> *Sweetheart,*
> *I'm sorry we're not going to see you this morning before you get married, but I'm sure you look beautiful. Your father had the bright idea to go to Pennsylvania, why there is beyond me, but it's a weekend away.*
> *I'll see you when you return from your honeymoon. Say hello to the family for me, and remember, you're doing the right thing.*
> *Love you,*
> *Mom*

Tanya tossed the note onto the table. She wondered if she had the nerve to back out of this thing since her mother wasn't home. Tanya's thoughts were interrupted by the sound of the doorbell. "Great." She said, "Why, today of all days, does Pam have to be on time?" She walked to the door to greet her friend. "Hey Pam."

Pam examined her dress. "You look great! Although I think you should act like you're happy."

"Why? I don't feel happy."

Pam shrugged. "I saw Gary last night. He was so excited…I really think he's into the whole marriage and having a family bit."

"Yeah there seems to be a lot of that going on around. I thought my mother was going to explode because she's so happy."

Pam looked around. "Where is your mother?"

"My parents went to Pennsylvania. I swear, the way my mother acted last night…" Tanya paused for a long moment. "I just thought she would've at least stayed around here long enough to make sure I went through with this."

Pam placed her purse on the kitchen table. "Well, maybe she didn't want to see her only daughter leave the nest."

Tanya leaned against the counter and hung her head. "What do you think would happen if I don't go through with this?"

"I think your mother would drag you to the nearest minister and forced you to do it." She scowled and said carefully, "Tanya, you do want to marry him…right?"

Tanya looked up and noticed the panicked look on her friend's face. "Oh…ah…yeah sure I do. I was just saying…you know…"

"Well it's too late now. I'll bet Gary's already at the J.P.'s office waiting for you." She glanced at her watch. "As a matter of fact we'll be late if we don't leave right now."

Tanya grabbed her purse and keys. As they walked through the door, her stomach clenched and a dull ache radiated through her abdomen. She closed the door and locked it.

Chapter 10

Pam parked in front of a long row of buildings lining Main Street. After turning off the engine, she turned to face Tanya. She was staring blankly at the door leading to the J.P.'s office. Pam said softly, "Are you alright?"

"Hmmm." She pulled herself out of her thoughts. "Oh…ah, yeah I'm fine."

Grasping the door handle, Pam gave it a shove with her elbow and smiled. "Well let's get this over with."

Tanya pushed her door open and stepped out. Standing on the sidewalk, she looked at the building and fought back her tears. Once Pam was standing beside her, Tanya pasted a smile on her face and said, "Well let's get going." They stepped toward the door.

Tanya's face lit up. "Hey I don't see Gary's car."

As they approached the door Pam said, "He said he was asked to park in the rear lot. I guess the J.P. didn't want to take up all the spaces in the front." She giggled. "Like that would happen. There are only three cars that I know of."

"Three? Who does the other one belong to?"

"Gary's best friend, Marcus. He's standing up for Gary, like I'm standing up for you." Pam held the door open all the while she took in the sad demeanor of her friend. She knew something was bothering Tanya, but she couldn't put her finger on it.

Tanya stepped into the dimly lit room and spied Gary standing in front of a huge mahogany desk. He was dressed in a dark blue suit with his arms in front of him, his fingers were laced. She noticed the J.P. standing behind the desk. He wore a white dress shirt and a black tie. She didn't think her stomach could clench any tighter…but it did. As she stepped forward Gary turned and smiled brightly. "Tanya, you look beautiful."

She lifted one side of her mouth in an ill-fated attempt to smile. "Thank you Gary, you look great too." She hung her head.

Gary stepped forward. "I don't know if you remember Marcus from the picnic we attended last month…"

"I remember. Hi Marcus, it's nice seeing you again." Gary scowled.

Pam stood beside Tanya and watched as Gary's face became tense. "Gary, is there something wrong?"

He glared at her. "Why would there be something wrong? I'm marrying a beautiful woman…"

"Oh never mind." She said interrupting him. "I just thought maybe you were nervous…that's all."

Gary shook his head and held his hand out to Tanya. She placed her hand in his and they both directed their attention to the J.P. Gary said, "We're ready when you are."

The man cleared his throat. "Alright if everyone will stand in front of the desk we'll get this started. I'm sure you want to get on with the celebration as soon as possible." He gestured with his hands. "I need the bride to stand on my right and the groom beside her. The two witnesses will stand beside your friends."

Pam stepped to Tanya's side and grasped her hand. She whispered. "Ready?" She smiled brightly.

Tanya began to tremble and her knees felt like rubber. She nodded and turned her attention to the man standing in front of her. As he started the ceremony Tanya felt Gary grasp her hand. She had a hard time breathing and wanted the stop the J.P. from continuing. She listened as Gary repeated his vows and said "I do."

Tiny beads of sweat formed on her forehead. Her knees threatened to fold and a tiny voice in her head kept repeating the words "Don't do it." She wasn't listening to the man standing in front of her; it was too hard to concentrate with everything that was rolling around in her head. She repeated the vows automaton like. Her voice didn't waver. She felt Gary squeeze her hand and she turned her head to glance at him. He motioned with his chin to look at the J.P. The man was standing, staring at her, waiting for an answer. The numbness she felt in her heart made it hard for Tanya to comprehend what she was supposed to do. Finally realization slammed into her head and she stammered over her words. "Oh...ah, I...ah do."

Gary smiled brightly.

The J. P. said with great enthusiasm, "I now pronounce you man and wife."

Gary wrapped his arms around her and held her tight. He kissed her passionately. After releasing his new bride, he turned to Marcus and said, "I'm the luckiest man alive."

Ten minutes. Tanya thought. *It only took ten minutes to give up my freedom...I just hope he's everything my mother made him out to be.*

Gary and Tanya said their good byes to their friends and Tanya promised to send Pam a postcard as soon as they arrived at their destination. Gary wrapped an arm around Tanya's waist and guided her toward the rear parking lot.

As soon as the car was in sight, Gary released Tanya and rushed to unlock the door. Instead of opening her door as he had done in the past, he quickly opened his door and climbed in. Tanya was rather stunned, but thought he just must be in a rush to drive the three hundred and fifty miles to her aunt's house. She heard the engine roar to life as she placed her hand on the door release, she felt the car start to roll. She quickly yanked the door open. She had to practically jump in just to prevent herself from being swept to the ground by the open door.

Once she was in and situated she glared at him. "What the hell was that all about?"

Gary returned her glare with his cold brown eyes. "Why were you flirting with Marcus?"

Confusion washed across her face. "What? I wasn't flirting with anyone. I was standing there minding my own business."

"Oh you were flirting." He growled. "And why the hell did it take you so long to say 'I do.' Why were you acting like you didn't want to be there?"

Tanya's stomach started to ache. She hated confrontation and she refused to say anything to cause her new husband's rage to escalate. "I'm sorry; I guess I was lost in the moment."

He scoffed. "Well my suggestion to you is to start paying attention. I swear your brain must be the size of a fucking pea."

Tears welled in her eyes and she turned her head and stared out the side window. She couldn't believe he could be so mean when just moments ago he appeared to be so happy.

"Let's get one thing straight. I'm your husband; I'm the boss in this relationship. I won't tolerate any more of your disrespect. When I tell you to do something...do it. If I tell you..."

Tanya turned to face him. "Look I don't know what you think you're doing, but I refuse to be bossed around. It's not too late to call this marriage off. Hell I don't think the ink is even dry yet."

Gary slammed on the brakes causing car tires to squeal behind them. "If you think for one minute you're going to play the annulment card you're sadly mistaken. We're married...we will stay married for the rest of our lives. You will bow down to me if I tell you too and you will..."

"I will kill you in your sleep if you keep up with this attitude!"

Gary pressed his foot on the gas. It felt like all the air had been sucked out of the car. Tanya refused to look at him so she turned her face to the window. After a few long moments of silence, Gary said softly, "I'm sorry, I didn't mean to upset you. I guess my jealousy escalated out of control."

"You had nothing to be jealous about. All I did was say hello to Marcus and now you're treating me like I went out and had sex with him."

"I know, you're absolutely right and I totally feel bad." He placed his hand on the nap of her neck and pulled her close. He gave her a quick kiss on the lips and returned to driving. "I love you. I really want you to know, I honestly love you."

Tanya didn't say a word. He entered the highway heading north.

Chapter 11

Tanya had always heard the first year of marriage was hard, but she never knew how hard. By the time they returned from their honeymoon she was ready to throw in the towel. Every day she had to cater to Gary like he was the king and she was some peasant. Although it saved a lot of arguing, Tanya was being worn ragged.

At the five month mark of her pregnancy, Gary was being nothing more than a bully. His mental abuse was causing severe stress and she was in danger of losing the baby. One night Gary came home from work in his usual bad mood. As soon as he entered the house he was screaming. "Tanya!" He rushed through the house and found her in bed sleeping. After creeping into the room, he knelt beside the bed, leaned in close and bellowed in her ear. "Get the fuck up!"

Tanya startled awake and in a panic she leapt to her feet. "What's wrong?" She scanned the room for a clue for the reason he was acting like the house was on fire.

"What's wrong?" He rose to his feet and loomed menacingly in front of her causing her to step back. "What's wrong? I'll tell you what's wrong. I'm sick and tired of coming home from work and seeing your ass lying in bed…that's what's wrong."

Tanya began to tremble. "Gary I can't work all day and stay up all night. Believe it or not, I'm human, I'm…"

He scoffed "Human is that what you call yourself?" He scrutinized her. "I suggest you get your ass into the kitchen and make my dinner."

I made dinner and left you a plate in the refrigerator." Tanya felt pain shoot across her abdomen. She pressed a hand against the wall to keep from falling.

"You call that dinner? I'm not eating that slop." Gary pointed to the bedroom door. His eyes were red and full of rage. He growled out his order. "Go out there and make me some fucking food."

Tanya took a step forward and the pain in her abdomen escalated causing her to place a protective hand on her bulging stomach. Another step and more searing pain caused Tanya to fold at the waist and crumple to the floor.

"Get up you fat fuck!"

Tanya moaned. Her body was trembling and tears began to flow. "Gary…" She tried to appease the raging man. She tried to get to her feet. Her only thoughts were how to calm Gary down enough to save the baby.

Gary stared down at his wife lying in a heap on the floor. His breath sawed in and out as he tried to calm his temper. After a few long moments he fell to his knees, wedged an arm around her neck and helped her to her feet. Carefully he sat her on the bed. Fear rolled through his eyes and Tanya could feel when he started to tremble. "Babe, what's wrong?"

She dried her tears with the back of her hands. "I have to go to the hospital Gary...there's something wrong with the baby."

Immediately he popped into action. It was as if nothing else mattered. He stammered. "Oh God...Oh Tanya, I..." He ran out of the bedroom through the kitchen and out the front door. Tanya slowly made it to her feet and through the bedroom door when Gary flew into the house and braced her. She leaned on him as they slowly made their way to the car.

Outside the car was idling and the passenger's door was open. He parked so close to the steps, there was barely room for the couple to stand. Gary eased her into the seat, slammed the door shut and rushed to get himself in the car.

By the time he crawled in he noticed Tanya's face was ash white. "Babe, we'll be at the hospital in five minutes. Just relax." Panic was in his tone. He shifted the car into first and sped out of the driveway.

Tanya thought he was going to break her hand he was holding it so tight. Every now and then she noticed him looking at her from the corner of his eyes. "Gary, you have to relax. Us getting into an accident isn't going to help."

She knew the moment his foot eased off the gas. After lifting her hand to his mouth, he placed a tender kiss on it. "Tanya we're almost there. I'm going to drive up to the emergency entrance to get someone to help us. I don't want you to move." His voice was soft and calming.

Tanya rested her eyes while he maneuvered the last few blocks to the hospital. "Gary, do you think the baby will be alright?" She opened her eyes and looked at him. His eyes welled with tears and his olive complexion was pale. He replied softly. "God I hope so."

Once they arrived, Gary turned into the emergency room drop off and laid on the horn. A heavy set man dressed in a navy blue security uniform approached the car, and yanked Tanya's door open. Goose bumps erupted on Tanya's bare skin when the cold winter air entered the car. The man leaned down and scanned her. "Can you walk?"

Gary glared at the man. "If she could walk I would've parked in the lot."

Stunned by Gary's harsh tone, the man turned his eyes to him. "I just need to know if I have to get a wheelchair."

Gary calmed infinitesimally. "Please…a chair would be great." He stepped out of the car and rushed to Tanya's side. Sitting on his haunches he clasped her hands firmly in his. "You're cold." He searched the back seat for something to put around her.

The security guard returned with a wheelchair and a warm blanket. "If you'd step aside, I'll help her into the chair."

Gary straightened and looked at the man. "I'll help her." Tanya placed her hands in his and he eased her to her feet. "How are you feeling?" Tanya shrugged. "Let's get you inside" He held her waist and she stepped toward the chair. The security guard locked the wheels and held the hand grips while Gary eased her into the seat.

"Go park your car. You can meet us inside…I'll have reception start the paperwork."

Once inside, Tanya explained the situation and immediately she was whisked to the maternity floor. Gary flew through the door a few minutes later, panting. "Is she going to be alright? He asked the nurse who was giving Tanya a shot. "We have the OBGYN doctor on call coming in to examine her." She glanced up from her work. "Do you know what caused the pain?"

Gary stilled, his jaw dropped and he stammered. "We…I…I guess…ah…it was my fault." The nurse scowled. "We were arguing and I…"

Tanya placed a hand on the nurse's forearm. "I was getting out of bed to go the bathroom when the pain started." Gary had a stunned look on his face. "I fell to my knees and he brought me in immediately." Tanya looked at Gary. "It wasn't the argument that caused this; I wasn't feeling well all evening and…"

The nurse eyed her suspiciously. "Alright, the main thing you have to do is calm down." She looked at Gary. "I don't want anything to upset her until the doctor comes. If you can't keep her calm, I'm going to have to ask you to leave."

Gary rushed to the side of the bed and grasped Tanya's hand. "I'll make sure she stays calm." The nurse walked out of the room giving Tanya one last glance over her shoulder.

By the time the doctor arrived the medication they had given Tanya was kicking in. Her abdominal pains were easing and she was finally able to relax.

"Mrs. Antonio, what were you doing when the pains first started?" The doctor pulled down the covers and lifted her gown while he listened to her explanation. He scowled when he felt her abdomen tighten. "I have to notify a technician, we'll need an ultrasound...I'll be right back."

Gary stared down at her. His eyes were rimmed with dark circles. "How are you feeling?"

"Fine." She said as she turned her head to look out the window.

"I didn't realize you were so stressed. I never meant to cause you any pain. Please look at me."

She turned to face him. "I'm tired of having to do everything. I think you should either take on some of the responsibility or just leave me alone...I do what I can, nothing more, nothing less."

"I love you Tanya, I'll do anything possible to make you happy. You don't have to worry about my dinner anymore...I ...ah will fix it." A tear trickled down his cheek. "Maybe I should have my mother come help you."

Tanya cringed. The last time she had a conversation with his mother, she called her a whore, and accused Tanya of trapping her son. There was no way she wanted that woman anywhere near her. "I don't want to sound mean, but I think its best we keep her out of this."

Gary was just about to say something when the doctor walked in. "I'm going to listen to the baby's heartbeat, then an orderly will come in to take you down to radiology."

He squirted a large dollop of clear gel on Tanya's lower abdomen and rubbed it around with the tip of his Doppler.

The quick steady sound of the child's heartbeat entered the room. Gary stared down at the small wand and asked, "Is that really the baby's heartbeat?"

The doctor smiled. "Yes it is, and it seems to be elevated."

"What does that mean?" Tanya said, worry in her tone.

The doctor looked from Tanya's abdomen to Gary then stared into Tanya's eyes. "It means whatever stress you went through has to stop…if you don't want to lose this child."

Gary ran both hands nervously over his short hair. "How long will she have to stay here? I don't want anything to happen to her or the baby."

After removing the wand from Tanya's abdomen, he wiped it off with a small white towel then handed the cloth to Tanya. "I think she'll be able to go home in a day or two. That all depends on Tanya's body. Let's just get her uterus to relax and in turn the baby will relax. I'm afraid to say it could take quite some time for her to get back to normal. She may have problems for the duration of the pregnancy."

Gary looked at Tanya. "You're saying if she gets upset, she could end up coming back here?"

"That's exactly what I'm saying. You have to make sure she remains calm. Next time you might not be so lucky…you could lose the baby and your wife."

Gary's legs were weak. He made his way to the blue plastic visitor's chair just before his knees gave out. He grasped Tanya's hands with both of his. "Oh babe, I don't care what it takes, there will be no way anything will upset you. I'll keep everyone away if I have too."

The doctor was sliding his Doppler into his pocket when a soft knock came on the door. As he stepped forward, the door slowly swung open. An orderly walked in pushing a wheelchair. "Dr. Morgan, I'm here to take your patient to radiology."

Dr. Morgan smiled at Tanya and clapped the orderly on the shoulder. "Let me know when the results are ready. Radiology knows this is urgent."

"Yes sir." The orderly said as he pushed the chair closer to the bed and waited while Gary helped Tanya into the chair.

Tanya returned home two days later. Gary had been at her side the entire time she was in the hospital just to make sure no one upset her. Once they were home, he only left her alone to go to work. Tanya loved the way

Gary's attitude changed, although she also wondered, how long would it last.

Chapter 12

Gary returned to his same old self one month after the incident that sent Tanya to the hospital. Even though he relapsed, she was happy she got a glimpse of the man he used to be. She made a solemn promise to herself to do everything in her power to make Gary happy. She refused to have her child raised in a divorced family. Although his harsh words stung, she considered them only words.

Between health issues and Gary's insistence, Tanya had to quit her job and became a full time house wife. Although she lost contact with the co-workers she had grown to love, she knew risking the baby's life was not an option.

The most upsetting thing for Tanya was when Gary told her she couldn't have her friends come around anymore. For the sake of saving an argument she told all her friends good-bye. Pam took it the hardest. She couldn't understand why Tanya was allowing Gary to control her.

Tanya's car broke down and Gary refused to have it repaired. It sat in the driveway for two weeks before Gary finally sold it. They didn't have a phone so every time Tanya needed to call someone she had to walk a half mile to the nearest pay phone. That alone made life very difficult for her as her belly swelled with child. Most days Tanya was lonely but she learned to take it in stride. Gary's temper terrified her so she did anything she could to keep it reined in.

Late one Friday afternoon, Tanya was feeling a little tired and listless, but Gary mentioned he had invited a few friends over on Saturday. She spent the entire afternoon cleaning everything. She scrubbed the kitchen floor on her hands and knees. After getting a second wind, and feeling full of energy, she washed walls, cabinets and scrubbed the bathroom. Tanya had hoped she'd get a compliment or two from Gary, so she continued to clean even though her body and the unborn baby was screaming stop. She scrubbed every nook and cranny in the small living space. By the time she was done the entire house was spotless and smelled of Lysol.

Standing in the center of the kitchen she smiled, not only was every surface clean, but all Gary's books and paperwork was neatly stacked on a shelf where Tanya stored her cookbooks. She wished she had the energy to stay awake until he returned from work, but the chores wiped her out. The pain she had grown accustomed to was escalating. Tanya knew she had pushed her body further than the doctors allowed, but she felt it was worth it just to make her husband happy.

Tanya was asleep when Gary came home, but that didn't last too long. Tanya was startled awake by the loud bellowing coming from Gary's mouth. "Get up you fucking lazy piece of shit!"

Tanya's eyes popped open. She rubbed the sleep from her eyes and looked up into Gary's raging face. "What's wrong?" Confused from being suddenly pulled from her peaceful dream state, she sat up straight in bed.

"Why don't you tell me what the hell is wrong?"

"I don't know. I was asleep when you came home."

"That's just it, you're always asleep. You do fucking nothing in this house while I work all night to provide for your fat ass."

Tanya rested a hand on her abdomen. The pain she had felt when she initially laid down was still there. "For your information, I'm not fat; I'm pregnant...with your child I'll add."

"Yeah, unfortunately I know that. I should've left you living in your mother's house...God knows you do nothing around here to make me happy."

Tanya climbed out of bed, placed a hand on her belly and growled. "For your information I cleaned this entire house tonight. I went to bed a half an hour ago because I wasn't feeling well."

He stepped forward forcing Tanya to step back until her back was pressed against the wall. His face was mere inches from hers when he snarled. "You fucking didn't clean the entire house. I just walked into the bathroom and noticed the tub isn't clean. So don't stand there telling me you cleaned the whole house when clearly you didn't." He turned and stepped toward the door. He muttered, "I suggest before you go to bed, you clean the bathroom. You're nothing but a worthless piece of shit." Tanya heard him slamming things around in the kitchen. He was growling to the top of his voice. "Why don't you get a fucking job? I should've left your ugly ass in the shit hole I found you in. Your mother and you belong together…you're nothing but two fucking worthless pigs."

Tanya slid down the wall, rested her elbows on her knees and covered her face with her hands. She sobbed. Sharp pains shot across her abdomen and Tanya panicked. She wanted to tell Gary but decided she had had enough badgering for one night. After rising to her feet, she placed a hand on her baby bump and proceeded to clean the tub.

The sound of Gary's snoring shocked her awake at seven o'clock the next morning. Pains continued to wreak havoc on her abdomen. *They never lasted all night before.* Tanya thought as she made her way to the bathroom. *I don't want to wake up Gary...he'll yell...call me inconsiderate...he'll call me pinhead or some other cruel name. I'll just have to suck it up.* A sharp pain shot across her abdomen. A hint of blood appeared on the toilet paper, fear made her hands tremble. Rushing to the bedroom, Tanya shook Gary awake. "We need to go to the hospital." She said with sheer panic in her tone. "Get up! I need to go to the hospital."

Gary mumbled, "Can't you wait a little while?"

"No Gary! We have to go now!"

He flung the covers off in a huff. "I swear to God, if you're fucking faking...."

"I'm not faking." She said as she pulled on her clothes. "I saw blood on the toilet paper this morning...we have to go!"

Finally listening to her words, Gary's face turned ash white. "Oh God...oh God...we have to get you to the hospital!" He pulled on his clothes and ran to the bathroom. After a few long moments he entered the kitchen. "Tanya I'm sorry about the way I treated you last night. I should've never said the thing I said...can you forgive me?"

She sat at the table, her head hung and tears streamed down her face. She started to stand when another strange sensation entered her torso. Her stomach became hard as a rock causing the sharper pain to become a throbbing ache. "Let's just forget about last night…" Gary wrapped an arm around her and helped her to the car. "I don't have a good feeling about this. The pain this time is far worse. Plus my stomach clenches…" Heavy sobs escaped her throat. "Oh Gary, I don't want to lose the baby."

His tone went from nervous to calming. "Just take it easy." He said as he opened the passenger's door and helped her in. "I'll have you at the hospital in ten minutes." He rushed to the driver's side. Tanya noticed he paused to stare up at the sky. She spied a glistening tear make its way down his cheek. He climbed into the car, slid the key into the ignition and gave it a twist. Not waiting for the engine to warm, Gary shifted to first and sped away.

They arrived at the hospital fifteen minutes later. At one point during the trip Tanya thought Gary was going to blow a gasket because traffic was moving so slow. He constantly told her he loved her and refused to release her hand. He was a nervous wreck by the time he pulled up to the emergency entrance.

After getting settled in a room, a doctor entered the room and examined her. He then had a nurse hook her to a fetal monitor and administer medication. Tanya stared at the ceiling while listening to the sound of the baby's heartbeat. Gary sobbed uncontrollably after the doctor stated the cause for the latest situation was extreme stress and the lack of rest. He then proceeded to explain, the need for Tanya to eliminate all stress and the importance of getting significant bed rest.

Once the fetus relaxed, due to the injection, Tanya's pain subsided. Another ultrasound was ordered and the doctor was comfortable the baby was developed enough should Tanya go into early labor.

Tanya delivered a healthy baby boy, Jason Antonio, three weeks premature. He was the apple of his father's eyes and a blessing to both sets of grandparents…even Gary's mother who swore the entire time Tanya was pregnant, the baby wasn't Gary's, stated the child looked just like his father.

Chapter 13

By the time five years rolled around, Tanya had been psychologically beaten down. She had no friends, her fragile ego had been shattered beyond repair and her husband grew more and more verbally abusive with every passing day. Fear alone caused her to stay. Not only the fear of what Gary would do, but also the fear of being told she was a failure. Tanya was depressed, her health suffered and her son also displayed signs of mental abuse.

Tanya sat at the kitchen table clipping coupons when the phone rang. Gary was downstairs working on a project, so she decided it was safe to answer the phone because the only people who called were their parents. She cleared her throat just before she lifted the handset and pushed the talk button. "Hello?"

"Hello is this Tanya Antonio?"

"Yes, who may I ask is calling?"

The woman on the other end of the line had a strong voice. "You don't know me, but my name is Lisa."

"What can I help you with Lisa?"

"I just think you should know your husband, Gary, has been seeing me for the past few months." The color in Tanya's face drained as she listened to the woman's words. "I just found out he was married and I didn't feel right allowing the relationship to continue. I broke up with him last night."

"Can you tell me why you waited all this time to contact me?"

"Like I said…"

Gary entered the room and asked. "Who's on the phone?"

"Hold on" Tanya said to the caller. She turned to face Gary.

Her eyes welled with tears and he yanked the receiver out of her hand. "Who is this?" he growled into the phone. After listening for a few brief moments he turned to Tanya. "You like talking on the phone?" He growled to the caller. "I suggest you fucking forget my phone number! If I were you, I'd stay away from me if you know what's good for you." He slammed down the receiver, grabbed the wire that was coming into the house and pulled it out of the wall. He then roughly swept the phone off the table and stomped on the base and the receiver. Bits of plastic flew in every direction. Wires were torn from the printed circuit boards and the small fiberglass boards were snapped.

Tanya watched as Gary completely destroyed the phone. Tears rolled down her cheeks and her entire body started to tremble. A knot formed in her stomach and the taste of blood entered her throat. "Gary." She said softly. "Was that woman telling me the truth?" She knew his words would say one thing, but she also knew, his eyes would tell another.

He stepped in front of her forcing her to step back. He pinned her against the front door and sneered, "You have to fucking ask that?" Spittle flew from his mouth. The whites of his eyes were blood red. His face was the color of a red plum. After placing a hand on either side of her he growled. "That woman doesn't know what she's talking about. She's nothing but a lying whore!"

Tanya pulled her eyes from his. Her knees became weak and threatened to give out. She turned her head away from him exposing her ear. He bellowed in the small appendage. "I DO NOT CHEAT ON YOU!" He eased away ever so slightly. "Did you fucking hear that? Or do I have to repeat myself? He slammed his fist on the wall causing a small dent in the sheetrock. "If you are that fucking gullible…If you can believe a lying tramp…" he flung his hands in the air out of frustration. "If you believe that bitch, then you are far dumber than even I thought was possible." He stepped toward the stairs that led to the second floor. "I suggest you clean up that fucking mess before Jason gets hurt." He pointed at the mangled phone lying on the floor. Tanya knelt on the floor and began picking up the pieces. Gary watched her from the head of the stairs. "Are you fucking stupid? Go get the trash can and toss the shit in it. Why the hell do I have to tell you everything?" He descended two steps. "Tanya, look at me." He said in a sarcastic tone. "Breath in...okay now exhale. You have to do that repeatedly in order to maintain your pathetic life. Got it, air in air out...don't forget. I'm going to take a shower and if you don't remember air in, air out you will die." He turned and walked into the bathroom. Tanya could hear his laughter from her position on the foyer floor.

Tears ran down her face. She frantically tried to come up with a plan to leave him. She knew the woman on the phone was telling the truth, she also felt if she didn't get away from him, he would eventually become physically abusive.

She waited until he had left the house, to visit his buddies, before she put her plan in motion. Her son, Jason had fallen asleep early so that gave her time to start packing before she woke him to leave. Quietly she grabbed a large blue suitcase from her bedroom closet and laid it on the bed. She tossed clothes haphazardly into the luggage while she muttered out loud. "I refuse to take any more of your bullshit. Let's see how you feel when you come home from a night on the town, and your family is long gone." Her anger made her work that much faster. Her ranting softened. Her pent up rage was dissipating. She wished she could be a fly on the wall when he returned home.

Chapter 14

Blue eyes filled with tears as Tanya continued to toss her clothes into the suitcase. Disgusted with herself for allowing her husband, to once again cause her insurmountable anguish. Not paying attention, she didn't notice when Jason entered the room. "Damn him for treating me like I'm some kind of animal." She muttered. "I can't believe he can say the things he does without a second thought about how I feel." Her long dark hair hung in her face and she pushed it away angrily.

"Mommy, are you going somewhere?"

Spinning around on her heels she stared down into the dark brown eyes of her son. "Oh Jason, What are you doing out of bed?"

"I couldn't sleep…daddy was yelling."

Kneeling down on the floor, she pulled him into a tight embrace and kissed him on the crown of his head. After easing him away, she quickly wiped a stray tear that escaped her eyes with the pads of her fingers. "I'm sorry you had to hear him."

He glanced from his mother to the suitcase and back again. Tears welled in his eyes. "Can I go with you?"

She smiled sadly. "Of course you can come. I would never leave my little man behind."

Jason dried his tears with the back of his hand. His short dark brown hair stuck up in every direction. "Is daddy coming with us?"

She bit her lip. Not really knowing what her child wanted to hear, she said softly, "No I don't think that's a good idea." She watched his face brighten. "Will that be all right with you?"

Jason nodded enthusiastically. "I'm glad he's not coming with us. I hate it when he yells."

Tanya straightened, placed a gentle hand on his head and stared into his eyes. "Why don't you go grab your suitcase and I'll help you pack it as soon as I'm done here." The little boy turned and stepped toward the door. "Oh and Jason, I need you to put a few of your favorite toys in your backpack…can you do that for mommy?"

From his hand dangled a well-loved teddy bear. He held it up to show his mother. "Can I take Charlie?"

A gentle smile crossed her lips. "Of course you can. We wouldn't want Charlie to be lonely…would we?"

"Do I have to put him in my backpack" his chin began to quiver. "He hates being in that bag."

"Do you think Charlie can sit nice in the car?"

He nodded. "He likes to look out the window."

Tanya smiled. "Then he can sit on the seat beside you."

Jason turned and ran out of the room "Yay! Did you hear that Charlie you can sit with me?"

Tanya returned to her packing feeling a little calmer after talking with her son. Once her bag was packed, she scanned the room for anything of sentimental value she wanted to take with her. Lifting a small frame from her bedside table she sighed. "I can't forget this." She said as she wrapped a photo of her parents in a thick hand towel. She laid the small bundle atop her clothes, flipped the lid closed and secured it with the zipper. After hefting the heavy bag from the bed, Tanya carried it from the room and placed it at the head of the stairs.

"Jason, are you almost ready?" She asked while entering his room. "We need to get going before your father comes home."

His small Thomas the tank engine suitcase was heaped with toys. Tanya put her hands on her hips. "Jason. You can't take everything you own."

"I know." He said as he swept an arm out. "I left most of my stuff. You said I could take the things I love." Tears welled in his eyes."

"I did say that, didn't I?"

"I need all this stuff." He said with certainty.

Tanya grimaced as she inspected the mountain of toys. "Do me a favor. Go to my closet and grab the big duffle bag…the one we use when we go camping." Jason darted out of the room in search of the bag. After removing the much loved toys from the bag, Tanya started to cry. "How could you force me to go to such drastic measures? Why does he have to pick and choose what toys he can take?" She said softly.

Jason returned to his room dragging the canvas bag and Charlie behind him. "Mommy." He said in a tone that made him sound years older. "Everything will be okay…please, don't cry."

Hearing her son's voice caused her muscles to tense. The last thing she wanted was her son to see her crying. She knew she had to be strong for him. Brushing the tears from her cheeks she smiled and sucked in a deep shuddering breath. "I know sweetheart, I'm just sad we have to leave like this."

He cautiously crossed the room and placed a small hand on her arm. "We can come back and get the rest of our stuff tomorrow."

She smiled even though she knew it would be days before she could return for the items she was leaving behind. Jason climbed on the bed and sat beside her. "Where are we going?" He asked as he rose to his feet and started jumping on the bed.

Tanya stood, grabbed her son mid leap and placed him firmly on the floor. "I think we'll visit grandma for a few days."

"Yay! I love going there. Maybe she'll make me some of those cookies with the frosting on them."

Tanya laughed in spite of herself. "I'm sure she will if you ask her nicely."

Tanya lifted the canvas bag from the floor where Jason dropped it, and stuffed it with her son's toys. Scowling down at the suitcase she realized he had only packed his shorts. She walked to his dresser and removed the clothes she thought he'd need and placed them into the luggage. She was glad it was summer; she knew if she had to pack winter clothes, he would need another piece of luggage. Once his clothes were secured in the suitcase, she swung the duffle bag over her shoulder, lifted the luggage from his bed and headed for the stairs.

Jason watched while his mother tried to carry everything at once. "Do you need help?" He asked as he happily swung Charlie beside him.

"I think I'll be all right. I'm just going to have to make two trips." She started walking down the stairs. "I do need you and Charlie to get in the car and get ready to leave."

He followed her down the stairs keeping a tight grip on the railing. "I can do that."

After loading the car, Tanya climbed into the driver's seat and glanced at her son's reflection in the rearview mirror. She turned to face him. "Are you and Charlie buckled in?"

He nodded. She slid the key into the ignition, gave it a twist and the engine roared to life. She backed out of the narrow driveway and headed to her mother's.

Chapter 15

Tanya pulled into her parent's driveway an hour and a half later. After parking the car, she turned and glanced at her son. He was slumped against the door fast asleep. One thin arm was wrapped protectively around Charlie. She couldn't help but smile when she eyed him. Her muscles tensed when she felt the door being yanked open. Quickly turning, she scowled then relaxed. "Dad, you didn't have to wait up."

Bob McBride's six foot frame stood beside the car. "Of course I did." He said as he held out his hand to help his daughter from the car. His dark blue eyes focused on hers for a brief moment. "I have to help you with Jason. Besides your mother has been worried sick ever since you called."

She pulled the trunk release. "Mom shouldn't worry…I'm a big girl." She walked to the rear of the car and started removing items and placed them gently onto the gravel driveway. "I hope she didn't cook."

"Now did you really think she wouldn't?" He said as he walked past her. "I swear the only time I get a decent meal is when you come over." He chuckled as he carefully eased Jason's door open. "Just leave the bags there honey; I'll come back to get them. Besides, your mother wants to talk to you."

Tanya's eyes filled with tears as she walked toward the front door. She placed her foot on the first step and was suddenly greeted by her mother. With arms spread wide Sherry welcomed her daughter home. "Oh Tanya, are you all right?"

She hugged her mother tight, and then eased away. Sherry dried Tanya's teary eyes. "Mom please. I don't need you to cater to me like I'm a three year old. I'll be fine, just give me a few minutes."

She grasped Tanya's hand and led her through the door. It wasn't until they entered the brightly lit kitchen when Sherry was able to see the condition her daughter was in. Tanya's puffy red rimmed eyes leaked the tears she had tried so hard to hide. Sherry bit her lip, cupped Tanya's face with her hands and kissed her cheek. "Why don't you sit down and relax while I set the table?"

Pulling out a chair, Tanya scanned the familiar room. "Mom when did you paint the kitchen?" She sat down in her chair.

Sherry paused in front of the granite countertop, one hand on a door pull of the oak cabinet. "I guess it's been a couple of weeks since I had your father paint. I was so tired of that hideous green. I swear your father has the worst taste when it comes to decorating a room." She smiled and returned to her task. "I think the ecru brightens the room…don't you?

Tanya placed an elbow on the table and rested her weary head in her hand. She inhaled deeply savoring the aroma of her mother's pot roast. "I don't know mom, I think I liked the green…it hid Jason's fingerprints better than this light color will." Tanya rose to her feet, walked to the sink, and washed her hand. She dried them on a paper towel and held out her hands. "Let me help you." She lifted the plates from the counter and placed them on the table, setting one in front of three chairs. She scowled while holding Jason's favorite Thomas the tank engine plate up. "Mom, Jason ate earlier. Besides it's after nine, he'll sleep for the rest of the night."

The two women heard a commotion and ran to the front door. Tanya grabbed the canvas bag from Bob's hand and placed it gently on the hardwood floor beside her. "You shouldn't have tried to carry everything all at once." She scolded as she reached for Jason's small suitcase. "I remember you always yelled at me whenever I did this same thing." She placed the luggage beside the bag.

Bob slid Tanya's heavy suitcase down the length of his leg and placed it on the floor beside the coat rack. "What the hell do you have in that thing, bricks?" He rubbed a knot that formed in the muscles of his lower back.

"I swear you and your mother are both the same. You both pack everything you possibly can into one bag." He smiled as he wrapped an arm around Tanya's waist and gave her a peck on the cheek. "Welcome home honey."

Sherry finished slicing the roast, lifted the platter of beef and vegetables and placed it in the center of the table. As she straightened, Bob pulled Sherry into his arms and gave her a quick peck on her lips. He released her and rubbed his hands together and moved to pull out a chair. He stared down at the platter like a hungry bear, he licked his lips and reached for the serving fork. A sharp tap hit his bare forearm and he turned his head to face his abuser. He scowled. "What'd you do that for?"

Sherry grinned. "I do believe you've lost every ounce of the manners I've taught you." She removed the fork from his hand and jabbed a thumb over her shoulder. "Go wash your hands." She said with a smile on her face. Sherry lifted and filled each plate and returned them to the table. While placing a potato on the last plate she asked, "Tell me sweetheart, did Gary give you a hard time when you left?"

Tanya mashed her potato with her fork. She kept her eyes glued to her plate when she answered. "He doesn't know we're gone. I packed after he left the house to go out with his so called buddies."

Bob returned to his seat and held up his hands. "See all clean." He lifted his fork and with a heavy hand he pressed the utensil firmly into the potato.

"What do you mean Tanya? Gary started an argument and then just left? Why would he do that?"

Tanya jabbed her fork into the small portion of beef she had cut. "He has a girlfriend mom." She placed the meat into her mouth and slowly chewed, savoring the flavor of her mother's cooking.

Sherry frowned. "You mean to tell me he started an argument just so he could go out with another woman? I'm sorry Tanya, but that doesn't sound like Gary." She scooped some peas onto her fork. "How do you know he has another woman?" She spilled the buttery vegetables into her mouth."

Tanya leaned back in her chair and wiped her mouth with a napkin. Her eyes filled with tears. "Regardless of what you think about Gary, he's not as nice as he comes across. He's always ridiculing me, he calls me names and he badgers me."

Bob looked up from his plate, with fork in hand he leaned forward. "What does he say?"

"Oh he says things like 'It's a wonder you know how to breathe with a brain the size of a pea.' He calls me worthless and incompetent. He threatens to take Jason away all the time. He always tells me I'm a poor excuse for a mother."

Sherry was stunned and Bob slammed his fist down on the table. "How dare he say that shit? Why didn't you tell us? Your mother and I would have hauled you out of that house in a heartbeat. There's no excuse for a man to treat his wife like a pile of garbage!" His deep voice seemed to echo through the house.

Sherry gritted her teeth while she listened to her husband speak. Once he was through with his spiel she softly said, "Calm down Bob. You're yelling isn't going to help matters." She directed her attention to Tanya. "Sweetheart, maybe he has a lot of things on his mind. I'm sure he's not the ogre you're making him out to be."

Tanya tossed her napkin on the table and rose to her feet. She glared down at her mother. "You only see the Gary he allows you to see. Believe me mother; he's far from the prince you thought I married. Whenever we have to go somewhere he starts yelling, screaming and throws things. It never fails every time there's a holiday or a party he goes berserk. I'm tired of being treated worse than the dirt on the bottom of his shoes. Gary's mean and vulgar. I have to think about Jason. He doesn't need to live around a man who's disrespectful and evil." She turned and stormed out of the room.

SHATTERED

Chapter 16

Tanya entered her childhood bedroom and sat on the edge of the bed. She kicked off her shoes and curled into a fetal position. Lying on her side, she rolled the feather pillow into a ball and rested her head. Tears spilled from her eyes and dampened her pillow case. A soft tap came on the door. Tanya sat up and wiped her eyes with the tips of her fingers.

The door creaked open slowly and one of her father's eyes peeked in. "Can I come in?" He said with a calming voice. He paused for a few moments while waiting for her reply. He pushed the door open and stepped and inside. Quietly he closed the door behind him and leaned against it. "I know things seem bleak at the moment, but rest assured things like this have a way of working themselves out. Your leaving him might be what Gary needs to realize he's been treating you poorly." He approached her bed and she made room for him to sit beside her. He wrapped a loving arm around her. "I hate seeing you like this. You're my baby girl and it breaks my heart to see you cry."

She leaned in close and inhaled the familiar scent of his Old Spice aftershave. "I know you do. I just hope Jason and I can get over the pain Gary caused."

Bob sat still. He clenched his teeth as he gathered the strength to ask his next question. "Has he ever hit you?"

Her head rested on his shoulder. She said with tears in her eyes, "No daddy, the pain he inflicts only leaves scars on the inside."

"Well, sometimes that pain is more difficult to bear. Bruises heal and fad with time. The damage done to a sensitive psyche is far greater than any beating you could endure." He caressed her back with slow even strokes of his big hand. "I'll never understand why some men treat their wives with disrespect." He shrugged. "Don't they realize when they force a woman to turn inside herself; is a piss poor reflection on them? Don't get me wrong, your mother and I had some doozies in our time, but we never attacked each other with hateful words. When we first got married I swear it was a battle of wills. We used to fight about everything from what we'd have for dinner, to the color of the paint on the walls. Never once did I call her stupid…I thought it lots of times, but that, like many other words never crossed my lips. I respect her far too much to call her names." He tried to lighten the mood. "Besides, I think she would've beaten me with the broom if I ever did. Your mother used to have quite the temper whenever she got riled."

Tanya rose to her feet and Bob followed suit. He opened the door and waited for her to cross the threshold. Standing in the hall with her arms crossed, Tanya turned to face her father. "Tell mom I'll be right down to help her with the dishes…I just want to check on Jason."

Bob placed his hand on her shoulder and gave it a gentle squeeze. "Take your time; I think she has my apron ready and waiting for me." Tanya laughed out loud, turned and headed to Jason's room.

Chapter 17

It was two a.m. when Tanya was startled awake by the chiming of her cell phone. After grabbing the device from the bedside table, she glanced down at the caller I.D. She growled. "Guess you're just getting home." She hit the talk button and pressed the phone to her ear. "Hello."

"Where the fuck are you?" Gary bellowed.

Tanya's body began to tremble when she heard his harsh words. "All of a sudden it matters where I am? Why now Gary...are you hungry?" She snapped.

"As a matter of fact I am! I suggest you get your fucking ass home and make me dinner...now God damn it!"

Her stomach clenched. Pain shot across her abdomen. She knew if she didn't go home she would have hell to pay in the morning. She sat up in bed, squared her shoulders and softly replied. "I'm sorry you're hungry. But I'm not going home. Jason and I are doing just fine right where we are." She sucked in a deep shuddering breath and forced back the tears that wanted so desperately to escape. "I have one suggestion for you; have your girlfriend cook your dinner."

Tanya had to pull the phone away from her ear. He spluttered, "I don't know what the fuck you're talking about. Of course the minute amount of gray matter within your skull of yours is barely enough to keep you alive without the added chore of logical thinking. Let me tell you this slow and in terms I'm sure even you'll be able to understand...I DO NOT HAVE A FUCKING GIRLFRIEND! Did you understand that?"

Tanya's hands shook uncontrollably. The tears she tried so hard to hold in flowed from her eyes. She licked away the acrid liquid from her lips, and stammered. "I'm...not..."

"Were the hell are you? I'll come and haul your ass home since you can't remember the way."

Gathering up a tiny bit of courage, Tanya swiped the tears from her face. Her voice was hushed and firm. "I'm not coming home and that's final!" She hit the end button and slid the device between the mattress and box spring.

Tanya flopped down on the pillows. She dried her eyes with a tattered tissue and angrily rolled onto her side. *I can't believe him.* She thought as she tried to ease her mind. Bile burned the back of her throat forcing her to sit up straight. She pushed her feet into her slippers, and padded to the bathroom. Silently she ranted about Gary's hateful words. *Does he really believe, him acting like that, will make me want to go home? Damn him for thinking I'm his puppet!*

When Tanya returned to her room, she heard the muffled chiming of her phone. Although she tried to relax, she knew in her heart Gary would terrorize everyone she knew until he found her. Rummaging through her purse, she found the prescription for the stomach pills and poured one into her palm. She then retrieved the prescription for valium and placed one of the tiny yellow pills beside the other. She tossed the medication into her mouth and forced them down her throat without as much as a sip of water. Tanya removed the phone from its hiding place. She noticed in the short time it took to use the bathroom, Gary had called six times. She turned off the phone and tossed it into her purse...*I'll deal with him tomorrow.*

Chapter 18

Tanya woke as soon as Jason leapt on her bed. With Charlie in hand he cuddled close to his mother and stared into her sleepy eyes. "Good morning mommy."

Tanya closed her eyes and mumbled, "Morning baby."

Jason waited for her to open her eyes again. A few brief moments passed, he placed a thumb on one of her lids and forced it open. "I know you're awake, because I can see your eye."

Tanya started to laugh. "Okay buddy, you caught me. I thought I could get a few more minutes of sleep, but I can see you're ready and raring to go."

Jason slid off the bed and started walking toward the door. "Do you think grandma's awake?"

She mumbled, "I doubt it." She lifted her head and glanced at her watch. "Oh Jason, it's only seven, can't you just lay with mommy for a little while?"

He inhaled deeply. "Grandma's making breakfast." He said excitedly. He ran out of the room and down the stairs.

Two hours later he returned. He crawled on the bed and placed Charlie beside his sleeping mother. He whispered loudly. "Mom." He pressed his small hands on her cheeks and leaned in close to whisper in her ear. "Mommy, grandma wants you to get up. She said she can't hold off the hungry bear any longer." Tanya opened her eyes and noticed Jason was scowling. "I didn't know grandma had a bear."

She wrapped her arms around him and squeezed. "I think she was talking about grandpa."

Jason slid off the bed and grabbed Charlie's furry paw. "Are you coming?"

"Yes." She moaned as she rolled out of bed. "Tell grandma I'm on my way." He ran from the room to deliver the message to Shelly.

Tanya entered the kitchen just as Shelly was placing a platter of pancakes and sausages on the table. Bob looked up and scowled. "Tanya, how are you feeling this morning? I heard you puttering around in the middle of the night…is everything okay?"

"Everything's fine dad. Gary called and woke me some time around two…he wanted me to go home to cook him dinner."

Shelly placed the syrup and butter dish on the table and sat down. "I'm sure he wasn't serious. Did he really believe you'd drive home that late just to cook him dinner?"

Yes he did. As a matter of fact he said if I didn't have…" she paused to think of his exact words. "He said and I'll quote, 'the minute amount of gray matter within your skull is barely enough to keep you alive without the added chore of logical thinking.'." She glared at her mother. "I'm sure if you'd really want to hear what he has to say, you can listen to the messages he left me after I hung up on him."

Shelly was dumbfounded. She placed a short stack of pancakes on Tanya's plate. "I don't understand. Every time I've spoken to him, he's always been so sweet." She shook her head as she poured warm maple syrup on her pancakes. "Maybe he's not feeling well. You know sometimes when I'm sick I get a little crabby."

From the corners of his eyes Bob glanced at his wife. A smile crossed his face. "A little crabby…I'd say your more like a mother bear protecting her young, when you're sick. Growling doesn't begin to describe how you speak to me…"

Tanya laughed out loud. "Oh dad, you don't have to exaggerate. I may not live here anymore, but I still remember how mom is when she doesn't feel well. You can't blame my husband's temper on an illness. Gary's a self-centered egotistical Neanderthal."

Shelly tried to suppress her chuckles with little success. "Sweetheart, calling the man you love a Neanderthal isn't exactly the nicest thing you can say…funny, but not very nice."

The conversation was interrupted by the ringing phone. Tanya's stomach clenched. Bob rose to his feet and grabbed the handset from the cradle, looked at the caller I.D. and clenched his teeth. "Sweetheart, it's your home phone."

"I don't want to talk to him...tell him I'm not here."

Bob pressed the talk button and put the phone to his ear. "Hello?"

The two women stared while Bob listened. "I'm sorry Gary, Tanya...well she's not here."

Shelly whispered, "Tell him she's at the store."

Tanya glared at her mother. Bob said, "No I don't think that's a good idea. Maybe you should cool off before you try talking to her." Another moment of silence, "All right, you do that. I'll see you soon...bye."

Tanya leaned back in her chair and crossed her arms. "What did he want?"

"He said he knew you were here...apparently he called everyone else and figured you'd come to us if you needed a place to stay." He stared into his daughters eyes. "I think he's learned his lesson...he was crying toward the end of the call. He's coming here to talk to you."

A burning sensation brewed in Tanya's stomach. She sat on her hands to stop them from trembling. Her knees bounced uncontrollably under the table. "Dad, why didn't you just tell him to leave me alone?"

"Tanya, I love you more than words could ever say, but I think you should at least hear him out. The man was crying for Christ sake. I don't know about Gary, but it takes a hell of a lot of heartache to make me shed a tear."

"I have to take a shower." Tanya stood and approached the stairs. She turned a looked at her father's solemn face. "I know you meant well, but I just wish you had asked me before you agreed to have him come here. I just want to say one thing…I won't be here when he arrives." She ascended the stairs. Shelly heard her daughter's soft sobs and her own eyes welled with tears.

Chapter 19

Gary pulled into the McBride's driveway at the same time Tanya was helping Jason into her car. She looked up when she heard the crunching of gravel. The look on his face caused Tanya's stomach to clench. Gary smiled and waved as he approached her vehicle. "Tanya, I need to talk to you...please."

She looked from Gary to the house and back again. "I don't have anything to say to you. Why don't you just go home and leave me alone?"

"Babe, I need you. Please hear me out. I promise I'll leave you alone if you just give me a chance to speak to you."

Jason turned and knelt on the seat to peer through the back window. The little boy scowled when he spied his father. He yanked on Tanya's blouse to get her attention. She glanced down and whispered, "What's wrong sweetie?"

"I thought daddy was supposed to stay home."

"Don't worry...why don't you go inside and stay with grandpa until I finish talking to your father?" He abruptly jumped out of the car and ran to the house. Bob swung the door open and waited for Jason to enter. He stared at Gary for a few long moments before he frowned and closed the door.

Tanya crossed her arms and leaned against her car. "Gary, I don't want to argue with you. I'm tired of being treated like an animal."

"Please Tanya, I need my family. I promise I'll never disrespect you again. You have to understand, I've had a lot of things on my mind. When I got home last night…" The lump in his throat made it difficult for him to continue.

Gary stepped closer and Tanya gasped when she noticed how disheveled he was. His wrinkled shirt hung loose around his muscular torso. His tear filled eyes were swollen from, what she thought was, hours of crying. Tanya nervously bit her lip. "What happened to you? You're usually very meticulous with your appearance. Today you look like you slept in your clothes."

He knelt on the gravel and grasped her hands. "Do you really have to ask? How do you think I feel…I got home last night to find my entire world crumbled in my absence?" He brought her hands to his lips and kissed them. "Please Tanya…please come home."

Tanya's heart melted. She crouched down in front of him and cupped his face with her hands. "I can't go back and be treated the way you've been treating me. I refuse to have

Jason living in a house where there's nothing but arguing." She stared into his pleading eyes. "I wish I could believe you, but that phone call..."

Gary interrupted. "I was scared. I searched the house for you and I honestly thought something happened to you or Jason...I panicked!"

Tanya straightened and stared down at the man who terrified her to her very core. She knew she had to try to work things out. She wanted more than anything to believe his words, but the memory of the phone call kept entering her mind. "You didn't sound panicked...you sounded enraged. How do you expect me to just forget all the hurtful words you've said in the past? Besides I know you have a girlfriend, I've noticed strange phone numbers on the bill. I've even called them and confronted the woman who answered. Not to mention the woman who called yesterday."

"Look at me. How can you stand there and believe I'd purposely hurt you? I swear on my mother's life, I never cheated on you. I love you...please tell me you'll at least think about coming home."

"Stand up. I can't have this conversation with you while you're kneeling on the ground."

He immediately rose to his feet. His five foot eleven frame towered over her. Feeling intimidated, Tanya took a step back. His dark brown eyes made her feel like they were penetrating into her very soul. She fidgeted nervously with the small gold locket that hung from her neck. Not willing to look into his eyes, Tanya stared at the gravel while she nudged the small stones with the toe of her shoe.

He placed a finger under her chin and guided her head until she looked at his face. He smiled and placed a gentle kiss on her unresponsive lips. Scowling he said, "What's wrong? I thought we made up…why are you acting like this?"

Tanya searched her brain because she honestly couldn't remember saying anything that would make him believe she had forgiven him. "What? Why in hell do you think I forgave you? I never said I forgave you."

"I can tell you'll forgive me. Your eyes tell me I'm already forgiven…all you have to do is say the words."

Tanya was totally confused. She wondered how he could possibly believe she had forgiven him. She looked into his eyes for a sum total of two minutes during their conversation. Gary stepped closer which made her feel intimidated. He smiled, but it wasn't the type that made her feel relaxed. If anything it made her fear him. "Gary, I want to believe…"

"Don't even think about it. I love you and I promise to treat you better…come home."

"I need a few days to think."

"I know." He said enthusiastically. "Today is Wednesday. I'll go home and paint the kitchen…" He stared down at her trying to get a reaction. "Remember you asked me a couple of months ago if I'd paint?" Tanya nodded. "Well I'll paint the kitchen and air out the house so it will be ready when you and Jason come home on Saturday…this will be like a mini vacation for the two of you."

A puzzled look crossed her face. She wondered how he managed to twist things around to make it sound like she had left to go on vacation. He wrapped his arms around her and held her close. He whispered, "I'm so glad you decided to come home." He leaned down and kissed her soft lips. While staring into her eyes he said, "I love you." He released her, smiled brightly and said, "I have to get going. I have to work tonight and then I'll take the rest of the week off. I'll start painting tomorrow." He took a step back, reached a hand in his pocket and pulled out his keys. "I'll see you on Saturday…I love you."

Tanya stood beside her car dumbdounded. She felt like she was lost in a fog. The conversation ran over and over in her head, and she couldn't figure out for the

life of her, how he managed to get her agree
to go home.

Tanya watched him climb into his car,
back out of the driveway and head home. She
crossed her arms and turned to the house, all
the while she replayed the confusing
conversation in her head.

Chapter 20

Tanya walked into the house straight into her father's loving embrace. "How'd he take the separation?" Bob whispered.

Easing away from him, she dried her eyes with the back of her hands. "I don't understand what just happened." She sniffed. "Somehow he manipulated the conversation and now I'm going home on Saturday."

Bob wiped a stray tear away with the pad of his thumb. "How did he explain himself?"

She gazed into her father's concerned eyes. "He told me he was sorry, he said he doesn't have a girlfriend and he's going to paint the kitchen while I'm here. He promised me he would change."

Bob wrapped an arm around her waist and led her to the kitchen. Sherry was loading the dishwasher. A metallic sound filled the air when the flatware clinked together. Bob pulled out a chair and Tanya slumped down on it. She placed her elbows on the table and covered her face with her hands.

Bob heard her muffled murmurs. "I just hope he's telling the truth. I would hate to have to put Jason through this again if things don't work out."

Sherry glanced at Bob and Tanya. "I take it things with Gary haven't changed.

Bob snapped his head around and met Sherry's eyes. "From what I understand, she and Jason will be going home on Saturday."

"Oh that's great!" Excited by the news, Sherry stopped what she was doing and rushed to Tanya's side. "Sweetheart, at least no one can say you didn't give up without a fight. You're trying to mend your marriage.., that's all anyone can ask for." Sherry slid her hand down the length of Tanya's hair.

Tanya removed her hands from her face revealing her puffy red rimmed eyes. "I guess you're right. I just hope Jason isn't disappointed. He was so excited when we left…God I hope I'm doing the right thing."

Bob walked to the counter, pulled open a cabinet and removed a glass. After opening the refrigerator he grabbed the bottle of orange juice and proceeded to fill the glass. Placing the bottle on the counter, he lifted the glass and delivered it to Tanya. "Here baby, drink this."

Tanya scowled down at the glass. "Dad, I can't have orange juice. My doctor told me to stay away from food and beverages with high acid content. I'm also supposed to avoid stress…like that's happening."

"Nonsense." He said snippily. "Orange juice never killed anyone."

"It's not the juice, it's the acid. I've been having problems with my stomach and if it persists, they'll want me to go for an endoscopy…personally, I don't want a camera shoved down my throat."

"Bob." Sherry scolded. "You should've asked her if she wanted juice. Now look…" She directed his attention to the glass. "…you've wasted an entire glass…"

Bob lifted the glass from the table. "Don't worry, orange juice never goes to waste around here. "He raised the glass to his lips and poured the tangy liquid into his mouth. He held up the empty glass. "See, no waste." He placed the glass in the dishwasher and returned to the table.

Sherry smiled. "Mr. McBride, you are a real piece of work."

Once everyone voiced their opinion, Tanya rose to her feet and walked up the stairs. She lay on her bed. Numb was the only way to describe the way she felt. Images of her life with Gary flooded her mind, as tears seeped from the corners of her eyes. Her stomach knotted, the bile started slowly flowing into the lower portion of her esophagus. Burning pain shot up her throat as the sour acid shot into her mouth. Tanya was forced to sit upright to relieve the reflux. The base of her skull felt as if it was on fire. Light headed and weak, Tanya was forced to chew an antacid.

A few long moments later the sensations began to ease. Tanya returned to her prone position and relaxed. The sound of Jason and her mother cooking in the kitchen below lulled her into a peaceful sleep.

Chapter 21

By the time Saturday rolled around, Tanya had fully accepted the fact she was returning home. The luggage had been stowed in the trunk of her car, and Jason, along with Charlie, was secured in the back seat. Standing in front of her parents, Tanya gave them a reassuring smile. "We'll be fine. I'll call you as soon as we get settled." She gave her parents a hug and climbed into the car.

Tanya turned to face her son. "All set Jason?" He nodded. "Is Charlie belted in beside you?

"Yes mommy." He looked down at the shaggy stuffed bear. "Charlie wants to know how long it will be until we're home."

She smiled and twisted the key. "You can tell Charlie we'll be home in about an hour."

He gave the bear a comforting pat on the head. "Did you hear that Charlie? We'll be home in one hour."

With each passing mile, Tanya's stomach tensed tighter and tighter. Soon she found herself reaching into her purse for the small container of antacids. A thick wall of tension surrounded her. Tanya's breathing increased and she was on the verge of hyperventilating. She realized the decision to return to her husband, was probably one of the worst choices she had made to date. Inhaling deeply Tanya slowly overcame the panic looming in her system. She thought, *I hope these feelings aren't telling me to turn around.* She peered into the rearview mirror and spied Jason's solemn face. "What's wrong baby?"

Jason simply shrugged. "Charlie wants to know if daddy's going to be nice to us."

"Oh sweetie, tell Charlie he has nothing to worry about. If daddy's mean, I'll take care of it."

"Like you did this time?"

Tanya bit her lip. She wasn't sure if her son meant she handled the situation as he had hoped, or if he was disappointed about going home. "Jason, can I ask you a question?"

He rested his elbow on the armrest. His hand was fisted and his chin was atop it. He stared out of the window. "What mommy?"

"Are you happy about going home?"

He lifted his chin from his fisted hand and met her eyes in the mirror. "I am if daddy's not going to yell anymore."

Tanya's grip on the steering wheel tightened. She knew there was no way she could promise her son his father wouldn't go back on his word. She pursed her lips. "Do you want to listen to your music?"

Jason returned to stare out the window. "I guess that would be good."

"I know what will cheer you and Charlie up." Jason eyed her in the mirror. "How about we stop for ice cream?"

A huge smile crossed the young boy's face. "Charlie says he wants chocolate…in a dish."

Tanya turned on her blinker and exited the highway. "I hope you and Charlie are hungry, because I know of a great place we can get real homemade ice cream."

She pulled into the parking lot, pushed open her door and slid out. She walked to the passenger side, yanked open the door and helped her son to his feet. As they walked into the ice cream parlor, Jason seemed gloomy. The normally happy little boy was reserved and appeared somewhat depressed. After receiving their order, Tanya followed Jason to a small table in front of the storefront windows.

He sat Charlie in a chair and pushed it close to the table. He proceeded to sit in the chair opposite his mother. Tanya handed him his bowl of chocolate ice cream and waited for him to speak. Jason scooped a small bit of the dairy treat onto his spoon and offered it to Charlie. Tanya scowled as the boy placed the spoon into the cup and pushed it away.

"What's the matter handsome?"

"Charlie's sad."

"Why is Charlie said?"

"Daddy said he was going to throw him in the trash. He told me Charlie was nothing more than a mangy piece of crap."

Tears welled in her eyes. She hadn't known Gary was tormenting Jason too. "Baby, look at mommy." He lifted his eyes and Tanya could see large tears starting to well in them. "You can tell Charlie there's no way I would ever allow your father to throw him in the trash. If he does, I'll personally fish him out." She watched as the little boy began to relax. "Jason, I want you to tell me if daddy ever does anything mean to you. I won't be able to fix things if you won't tell me…do we have a deal?" She stared at him waiting for a response.

Jason pulled his bowl closer, picked up the spoon and again tried to feed the well loved bear. His eyes sparkled. "Charlie likes the ice cream." Jason started eating his favorite treat.

Tanya quietly watched her son as he ate. "Jason, has daddy ever hit you?"

He shook his head. "No, he's not mean to me he's just mean to Charlie."

"Has he ever hit Charlie?" She thought Jason might have been using Charlie to tell her about a problem he was having.

"No, he just yells at him. He told me Charlie was a girl's toy. He told me only babies play with stuffed animals."

"That's not true!" Tanya said a little louder than she intended. "I know lots of kids, girls and boys, who love stuffed toys. Besides Charlie's more than a toy...he's your friend."

"Yeah I know a few kids that have friends like Charlie. Tommy Lancaster brings his stuffed tiger to school. He told me, Douglas, that's his name, protects him from the devil."

Stunned was the only way Tanya's expression could be described. Her eyes widen with surprise and her jaw dropped. Regaining her composure she placed her spoon beside the empty bowl in front of her. "Why does he think he needs protection from the devil?"

Jason continued to eat. He shrugged and mumbled between bites. "I don't know, but sometimes he comes to school with bruises on his face. One time he even had a broken arm. That time he told me he had to fight the devil to save his mom."

Oh God. Tanya thought, *the devil must be Tommy's step-father.* Tears welled in her eyes. "Did Tommy ever tell you Douglas beat up the devil?" Tiny beads of sweat began to form on her forehead, and her heart felt like it weighed twenty pounds.

"Yeah, he said the devil was sent back to...ah..." He stared up at his mother. "You won't be mad at me if I tell you where the devil went will you?" At a loss for words, Tanya simply shook her head. Jason whispered, "He went back to H. E. double toothpicks." He quickly covered his mouth with both hands.

Tanya smiled. "It's okay honey, you didn't say anything bad."

"I thought it was a bad thing to say, because Tommy had to sit in the corner when Mrs. Franklin heard him say it."

"No sweetheart, it's not bad. I don't know why Mrs. Franklin sat him in the corner, but it wasn't because of that."

They finished their ice cream and headed home. Tanya's heart ached when she thought about the little blonde haired boy from Jason's class.

Chapter 22

When Tanya pulled into the driveway, she was mentally exhausted. The past few days took a toll on her, and the latest conversation with Jason still weighed heavy on her heart. She was surprised when she didn't see Gary's car in the driveway. She assumed he must've gone out for something to eat.

Jason ran to the front door, with Charlie flopping beside him. He stood on the porch and waited for his mother to open the door. She smiled at her son while she made her way to the front door. The canvas bag of toys was slung over her shoulder and his small piece of luggage hung from her hand. She walked up the three steps to the porch, slid the key into the lock and pushed the door open.

Tanya stood in stunned silence as she took in the horrendous mess that greeted her. In the center of the foyer stood two saw horses with an eight foot length of plywood strategically laid on top. There was a five gallon paint bucket underneath and a metal paint tray covered with dried yellow paint. A roller rested inside the tray that was also covered with the same hideous yellow as in the tray. "Great." She said as she placed her burden on the floor in the corner of the room.

As Jason stepped through the door he stared with amazement in his eyes. "Wow! Daddy's painting. I wonder if he'll let me help!" He immediately ran over to the paint tray, grasped the roller by the handle and lifted it. Up came the roller with the tray securely attached.

Tanya frowned. "Jason put that down!" She scolded as she walked from the foyer into the living room. Tears welled in her eyes when she spied the heap of clean, un-folded laundry on the sofa. "What the hell has he been doing? How could someone just leave laundry in a ball on a sofa?" She sorted through the pile and found tissues that had obviously been left in Gary's pockets. "He didn't even empty his pockets before he washed the clothes." She shoved the pile aside, sat on the sofa and started folding.

After folding and neatly stacking the laundry, she glanced down at the pile of clean tissues. She shrugged and began folding them while she thought; *he must have wanted to save these since he washed them. If I throw them away he's bound to yell and scream at me for disrespecting his personal property.*

Once the laundry task was completed, Tanya hesitantly entered the kitchen. She knew since the living room had been turned into laundry central, then the kitchen must have also been transformed.

The look on Tanya's face as she entered the large kitchen was nothing less than a Kodak moment. Blue tape had been stuck around the perimeter of every window and doorway. A blue plastic tarp was spread on the floor and displayed large splatters of white paint. Every cabinet door had been removed, and propped against the back door. One side of the double bowl sink was piled with dirty dishes, while the other had paint rollers and brushes that had been partially cleaned. She picked up one of the rollers and grimaced. Staring down into the filthy stainless steel sink she spied a white ring where the roller had been standing. Tears trickled down her cheeks, her stomach twisted into a knot and her anger meter was spinning out of control.

She didn't want to run from the house screaming, knowing the neighbors would call the police. They'd have the half crazed woman sent to the asylum for the criminally insane; instead she pulled on a pair of rubber gloves and started to clean.

Tanya was cleaning the counter when Gary walked in. He pressed his muscular body against her back pinning her to the counter. He kissed her neck and whispered. "Welcome home sweetheart."

Fire burned in the pit of her stomach. The anger that built up inside her, exploded.

Tanya pushed him away and spun around to face him. Her raging temper turned her usual pale face to a deep red. Her eyes were puffy and bloodshot from crying. Holding a dripping sponge in one gloved hand and a disinfectant spray in the other she lashed out. "Welcome home! Is that what you call this? I've been here for three hours trying to clean the mess you made! How dare you waltz in here thinking everything is hunky dory, when in reality, you showed me just how much you respect me. I guess if I were standing in your shoes I'd think everything was just perfect too." She spun around and returned to her cleaning.

"What the hell crawled up your ass? You're acting like I haven't done anything while you were away." He proudly swept an arm out. "I've been working on this kitchen for three solid days, and all you can do is bitch."

Tanya tossed the sponge in the sink and ripped of her rubber gloves. She glowered at him. "Gary I'm far from the idiot you think I am. I know for a fact you haven't worked in this house for a couple of days…and do you know how I know this?"

The veins on Gary's forehead surfaced and bulged. His dark brown eyes turned to hers. Chills ran up her spine when she realized she had pushed him a little too far. Her aching stomach threatened to expel its contents.

Tanya's face went from anger to fear in the time it took for Gary to jump off the sanity wagon. "I worked my fucking ass off and all you can do is ridicule me!" Gary growled as he tossed his hands in the air. "I don't know what you think I've been doing, but I assure you, I've been working nonstop to get this kitchen done…for you! And here you are, complaining about a little cleaning."

Tanya knew he was far angrier than he had ever been. She wasn't willing to push the issue any further. She watched him pull a beer from the refrigerator, twisted the top and tossed the cap onto the counter. She eyed the small cap as it bounced off the backsplash, rolled and finally hit the floor. It was as if her eyes had been glued to the small piece of metal.

Being in a trance like state, she didn't realize Gary was talking until he waved a hand in front of her face. "Hello! Is anyone home?" He said sarcastically.

Tanya pried her eyes away from the cap and looked up at the raging maniac. "Sorry, I was just thinking."

"Well don't think too hard, I wouldn't want you to kill off any of the five working brain cells you have." He laughed; it was a terrifying laugh that sent chills up her spine.

She pushed past him, walked into the foyer and grabbed her purse. She rummaged around the bag and pulled out the bottle containing her stomach pills. Tanya opened the bottle, removed a pill, tossed it in her mouth and swallowed.

Gary stood in the doorway between the kitchen and the foyer watching her every move. He watched her return the small brown bottle to her purse. "Tanya is there something wrong?"

She couldn't believe her ears. He went from a raging animal to a caring husband in the short time it took her to take a pill. Not daring to look at him, she held her eyes on the purse in her hand. Beads of sweat formed on her forehead as she felt the bile erupt and wash her mouth with the foul tasting liquid. "It's nothing for you to worry about." She said while pushing a stray strand of hair behind her ear.

He approached her slowly. "Babe, why do you have a prescription?"

Tears welled in her eyes and she continued to avoid his gaze. "It's nothing. I just have a few stomach issues."

"Thank God, I thought there was something really wrong with you." He sipped his beer as he brushed past her. Not giving her a second glance.

Chapter 23

Sunday morning Tanya woke to the sound of Gary's bellowing voice. "God damned fucking piece of shit!" She heard something slam against a wall and drop to the floor. *What the hell. Why is he tossing wood around? He wasn't working on anything that had to do with wood. He's only painting.* She thought.

She climbed out of bed, pulled on her robe and stepped into her slippers. After taking care of business in the bathroom and listening to more ranting, Tanya slowly crept halfway down the stairs. Once she reached the area where she could peer into the kitchen, she sat down and watched while he muttered. "Fucking bitch." He was in the process of rolling paint onto a wall when his hand slipped and the roller hit the center of the door. His back was to her, Tanya felt comfortable enough to slide down a couple of steps.

She watched as he swiped the wet paint with a rag, flung it on the floor and growled. "I can't believe I have to fucking spend my time doing this shit. I should have left the fucking idiot at her mothers."

Tanya scowled. She debated whether or not to confront him, or if she should stay put and continue to listen. The idea of confronting him was quickly erased from her mind when her stomach twisted into a knot. She knew if he found out she was watching him he would lash out. Her decision was made; she would go to the kitchen and offer to help.

"Good morning Gary." She said softly.

He turned to face her, roller in hand and paint dripping onto the blue tarp. The heavy plastic crackled below his feet. "Oh...ah good morning hon. How did you sleep?"

She couldn't believe her ears. Moments ago he was cussing, now he was sounding sweet and innocent. "Do you need any help?"

He scowled. "If you want to help, you're going to have to change. I don't think a bathrobe is the best item to wear while painting."

She released the breath she'd been hold, thankful he didn't lash out at her with his cruel words. "I'll be right back."

She turned, ran up the stairs and changed into a pair of old jeans and a beat-up tee-shirt. She smiled. Wow maybe he'll be in a good mood...maybe we can go an entire day without an argument. Tanya raced down the stairs and into the kitchen. "What can I do?"

He was applying paint to the roller. "Grab a brush. I need you to do the cutting in." He looked up, bit his lip and asked, "Do you know what cutting in means?"

Tanya scowled. "Of course I do." She looked around the room in search of the paint brushes. "Gary, where are the brushes?" It was that very question that changed the tempo for the day.

"What the fuck! I thought you wanted to help. If I knew I was going to have to stop what I'm doing to get you a brush... never mind, I'll get it." He roughly tossed the roller into the paint tray, causing the paint to splash onto the tarp. He then stormed to the basement door and flung it open, nearly hitting her in the process.

Tanya heard him mumbling as he slammed things around. Finally the noise and the growling stopped and she relaxed against the counter. Five minutes passed and Gary still hadn't emerged from the basement. Concerned, Tanya stepped forward. As she approached the head of the stairs she spied him. Brushes in hand, he was breathing heavy and poised to climb the stairs. *What the hell happened?* She wondered as she placed her right foot on the first step.

Her breathing accelerated and her stomach twisted when she noticed the look on his face. Rage was the only way to describe his reddened face. His teeth were clenched, sweat glistened on his face and his eye looked as it if they were going to pop out of his head. Tanya gasped and backed away from cellar door. Fear caused her heart to race. Her hands trembled and the bile in her stomach churned. "Gary, are you all right? "She asked with hesitation in her trembling voice.

"I'm fine!" He growled as he clomped heavy footed up the stairs. "Next time you decide to help…" He stared into her eyes and Tanya knew he was desperately trying to rein in his temper. He handed her the brushes. "There's an old plastic container in the foyer under the work area. Grab it and I'll fill it with paint."

Once the container was ready, Tanya grabbed the stepstool and placed it in front of the cabinets. She decided she would work her way around the far side of the room and stay as far away from Gary as possible. Classic rock played from the black boom box Gary had placed on the stove.

An hour passed and she was cutting in around the cellar door when her favorite song start to play. She was painting to the rhythm, tapping her feet to the music and softly humming along. Absentmindedly she started to sing…out loud. She loved to sing. Many people in the past had complimented Tanya's singing voice. She had won a few contests but she never considered perusing a career.

"Tanya, shut the fuck up!" Gary bellowed. "No one wants to hear you're your fucking yap!"

Immediately she clamped her mouth shut. She continued with her painting task not daring to utter another sound.

Chapter 24

After the kitchen had been painted and the supplies stowed, Tanya took a hot relaxing shower. She was mentally drained and wanted nothing more than to get through the rest of the day without complications.

She hadn't dared to speak to Gary out of fear he would lash out at her again. After much internal deliberation she finally broke the silence. "Gary?"

He was just entering the kitchen after being in the basement. "What hon.?"

"Are you hungry?"

He smiled brightly. "As a matter of fact I am. What did you have in mind?"

"I thought I'd go to the store, grab a couple steaks and I'd cook outside." She didn't want to cook in the kitchen until the fresh paint was completely dry.

Gary stared down at the floor as if deep in thought. "That sounds great. I'll take a shower and go with you. Maybe we should pick up Jason on the way."

Tanya shook her head. "Your mother said she wanted to keep him until Tuesday. She said something about taking him to some carnival in town."

He stretched his arms over his head and yawned. "That's right I forgot all about the carnival plans. Okay, go to the store; I'll take a shower and light the grill. By the time you get back the grill will be hot and we can start cooking." Gary slowly approached her. "I'm really sorry I yelled at you. I didn't mean to...I was...just feeling over whelmed. Thank you for helping me with the painting." He kissed her tenderly. "I love you."

Tanya was totally at a loss for words. He had rarely apologized for anything, and he was standing in front of her acting all sweet and sincere. She didn't know if he thought she was on the verge of leaving again, or if he really was sorry. She kissed him back. "It's all right, I know how stressful it is to have a huge task to do and thinking you'll never get done."

He held her close. "I really am trying. I want to make you happy. I never want to have to come home to an empty house again."

She stared into his eyes looking for anything that would tell her he's being honest....nothing was there. She nodded and eased away from him. "I'll be back in about fifteen minutes." She grabbed her purse and walked out the door.

When Tanya returned, instead of going into the house through the front door, she walked to the backyard. She thought she'd throw the steaks on the grill, then go inside to make a salad and grab the plates. She was disappointed when she discovered the grill hadn't been lit. With a heavy sigh, she placed the bag on the patio table and proceeded to light the grill.

As she walked through the back door, she heard Gary talking to someone. "…I can't, I told you my wife is being a royal bitch." Tanya's stomach tightened. Not daring to make a sound, she closed the door softly and stood stalk still. After a short period of silence he said, "Look Tammy, I'll try to get away after dinner. I'm sure the bitch will be tired after painting all day."

Tanya's eyes started to tear. She didn't know what to do. Her knees felt like rubber when she finally decided to confront him. Slowly she crept toward the living room. She stood just outside the arched doorway and peeked into the room. He was sitting on the sofa with his dick in his hand jerking off. Tanya had to lean against the wall to keep from falling.

Finally after a few more long agonizing minutes she heard the undeniable sound of his climax. He said after a brief pause. "Thank you for helping me take care of myself…I can't wait to see you." His faced drained of color when Tanya walked into the room.

"I have to go." Gary hung up the phone and stared at Tanya. She could tell by the look on his face his mind was trying to figure a way out of the situation.

Tears spilled from Tanya's eyes and made a slow trek down her cheek. She was to hurt to say anything that would force him to lie, so she said, "You might want to turn off the grill." She turned to walk out of the room, paused with her right foot on the first stair and continued, "The steaks are on the deck." She walked slowly up the stairs, closed and locked the bedroom door.

Tanya was proud; she had managed to hold in her heavy sobs until she was in the privacy of her room. Once the door was closed and locked she flopped down on the bed and had herself a good long cry. She knew Gary was downstairs trying to figure out a lie he could use to dig himself out of the huge pile of shit he had buried himself under.

She gathered her courage, grasped the suitcase containing her clothes, unlocked the door and stepped into the hall. Thankfully Jason's luggage was also packed, so she swung the canvas bag over her shoulder lifted both pieces of luggage and headed down the stairs. She didn't stop to say a word to him; she just kept walking out the front door and loaded her burden into the trunk.

She climbed into her car at the same moment Gary flew out of the house. *Two seconds.* She thought, *I only needed two more seconds.* He yanked the door open and stared down at her.

"It's not what you think…please Tanya you have to hear me out."

If her eyes could have shot daggers he would have been dead. "Oh, and what do you think I saw and heard?"

"Baby, please, you have to give me a chance to explain."

She crossed her arms and he sat on his haunches beside the car. "All right, what do you have to say for yourself?" Her stomach was twisted so tight she thought the knot would never release. Every muscle in her body tensed when he place his hand, the one he used to pleasure himself, on her arm. She glared down at it and he quickly pulled it back.

"I can explain…"

"Well then, do it. I have someplace I need to be."

"Baby, I was just talking to a friend…and…"

"Let me spare you the time. You were talking to your friend and your dick just happened to fall in your hand. 'Tanya you don't know what I've been going through for the past few days'…Is that about the size of it Gary?"

He swallowed hard. "She means nothing to me. I swear I'll break it off if you'll just reconsider."

"Gary." She said with arrogance in her tone. "I gave you a chance…I didn't cut your dick off when I caught you. Maybe you and…what's her name can have a beautiful life together." She slid the key into the ignition and twisted it. "Now if you would be so kind as to remove your lying ass away from the door, I'll be leaving." She placed her left hand on the door and pulled. He didn't budge.

"Sweetheart, baby, please…" He played the crying card. "I'm nothing without you."

Tanya refused to look at him. "Gary, I'm warning you…get away from the door. I swear I'll run you over if you don't move." She shifted the car into reverse and released the break. The car started to roll.

Gary straightened and stepped away from the car. "I'll prove to you…I'll prove you're making a mountain out of a molehill." He shouted as she drove away from the house.

Chapter 25

Tanya was lying on a chaise lounge watching Jason play in a small pool when she heard her mother calling to her from the patio door. "Tanya, you have a phone call."

"Who is it mom?"

Her mother's voice was tense when she replied. "It's Gary. He says he needs to talk to you."

What the hell does he want? I've had two weeks of peace and quiet...now this, has to ruin it. "Tell him I'm busy." Tanya growled.

"I already told him you weren't."

"Thanks mom." She muttered while climbing out of the chair. "Jason I need you to get out of the pool until I come back out.

"Awe mom!" Disappointment showed on his face.

"Jason you can stay in the pool. I'll come out and watch you." Sherry said as she slid the screen door open.

Tanya stepped onto the patio and glared at her mother. "Where's the phone?"

"It's on the table." Tanya pushed past her and slid the screen door closed. "Take your time dear, I'll stay with Jason until you get back."

Tanya nervously paced around the kitchen, shaking her hands, and hissing through her teeth. Deep growls escaped her throat. Spittle flew from her mouth and landed on the floor. She hadn't expected Gary to call her; he knew he was caught with his hand in the cookie jar so to speak. There was nothing he could do or say to change the way she felt about him. Leaning over, her hands on her knees and her long dark hair hanging loosely, Tanya tried to relax.

After picking up the hand set, she rudely said, "What do you want?"

"Tanya." He pleaded. "I just want to talk to you. I need to see you...please baby."

She crossed her free arm over her abdomen and rested her elbow in her hand. She glared at the floor. "Gary, I think you did enough to me. I don't think talking will help our situation...face it you screwed up."

Heavy sobs entered her ear. "Please...please I can't live without you. I just want one chance to explain." His pleading was starting to make her icy façade melt. "Please baby, one chance. That's all I'm asking for."

While glaring at the floor she nervously bit her lip. "Tell you what. I'll meet you at Anthony's pizza place in one hour. If you're late you might as well just turn around." She glanced up at the clock. "I'm going to make it nice and simple for you. It's one forty-five now, so if you're not there at two forty-five I won't be either…is that understood?"

Gary's sobs softened. "I'll be there. Please, please promise you'll wait for me."

"Two forty-five…that's final." She hit the end button. Slammed the handset into the cradle and stormed out the back door.

Sherry was kneeling on the ground beside the pool when Tanya approached. She looked at Jason then turned her stare to Tanya. "Mother." Tanya growled, hands on her hips and fuming. "I need to talk to you." She glared at Jason. "Sweetie, I need you to get out of the pool until I'm finished talking to grandma."

"Are you going to yell at her?" Jason stood stock still with the exception of his fidgeting fingers. His skin was covered with goose bumps and his teeth chattered.

"Jason, you're cold. Come here, I'll wrap your towel around you so you can warm up." She stretched the towel out straight and waited for her son to approach. After wrapping the towel around him, she kissed his cheek. "I'm not going to yell at grandma, I just have to discuss something with her. Now be a good boy and sit in the lounge." Jason did as he was told. Sherry smiled nervously and followed Tanya into the house.

Tanya leaned against the granite countertop and released an exasperated sigh. "Mom, I asked you to tell Gary, when he called, I didn't want to speak to him. You know how much I hate confrontations and he's the most confrontational person I've ever met. Now he wants me to meet him so he can…" She crossed her arms and glowered. "Oh mom, I know when I see him he's going to say everything I want to hear. He'll tell me he's sorry and…"

Sherry held out her arms and Tanya stepped closer. She wrapped her arms around her and caressed Tanya's back. "Sweetheart, I've talked to Gary and I know he loves you. He made a mistake…everybody does. I know what he did was wrong, but I also know everyone deserves a second chance."

Tanya sniffed and eased away from her mother's arms. "But he cheated on me. He called me a bitch. How am I supposed to forget about all the horrible things he's said and done?"

Sherry grasped Tanya's hands, led her to a chair and sat her down. Kneeling down in front of her daughter Sherry explained, "I know you've had a rocky marriage, and I also know deep down in your heart you love him. You know you never give anything up without at least giving it your all. Please, I'm asking you to hear him out. Listen to his words and come to an agreement, you can both live with."

Tanya's tears flowed in rivulets down her cheeks. She took a deep shuddering breath.

"I'll listen, but I'm not guaranteeing anything."

Sherry stood and brushed her hand down the back of Tanya's head stopping at the nap of her neck. "That's all I ask…listen and then decide if you can live with what he has to offer." She walked to the counter and pulled a tissue from the box and handed it to her daughter. "Here, dry your eyes, and get ready. Jason and I'll make cookies while you're gone…he just loves the ones with the icing."

Tanya scoffed, "I know he does. He always asks, whenever we're coming for a visit, if you'll make cookies with him…he loves to help you cook."

Sherry held out her hands and Tanya took them. She pulled her to her feet, embraced her tight and gave her daughter a tender kiss on her cheek. "Now go get ready to meet your husband."

Tanya nodded and ran upstairs to change.

Chapter 26

By the time Tanya drove the forty-five minutes to Anthony's she was an emotional mess. Her stomach acid was waging war on her throat. Taking her prescription and consuming an entire roll of antacids did nothing to calm the beast within. *I have to remain strong.* She thought as she parked her car. *You can't let him manipulate you. You're going to go in there...*A knock on her window interrupted her thought.

The face staring at her through the glass was nearly unrecognizable. The eyes that stared back at her from the familiar face somehow lost their life. The life that once filled the soft dark brown eyes looked almost dead. His natural olive completion, that used to show hints of rose on the cheeks, had been washed of color. She gasped.

Gary pulled open her door and helped Tanya to her feet. He pulled her close, buried his face in her hair and sobbed. "Oh God, oh God...I've missed you so much." He said through his tears. "Thank you so much for meeting me."

Tanya eased away from him. She stared into his eyes, worry flooded her body. "Gary, why…" she placed a hand on his cheek. Her eyes filled with tears. "Oh Gary…"

He pulled her back into his arms and held her as if he would never let her go. "Baby, I know I've said this before, but after living without you for two weeks, I am positive I can't live without you." Heavy sobs escaped his throat.

"I think we need to talk." She whispered. "Come on, sit in the car. I don't want you going inside looking like this."

Once Tanya climbed into the driver's seat, Gary slowly made his way around the car. She watched him as he pulled open the door and crawled in. He twisted his body, leaned his back against the door and stared down at his fidgeting hands. "I have so much to regret…all the things I've said to you and all the things I've done…" Tanya's attitude changed from disgust to compassionate in a matter of seconds. He looked up at her. "Tanya, there's nothing I can say…I don't know how to express the…the reasoning behind the shameful way I treated you. I swear if you give me another chance to prove to you…I swear I'll cherish every moment. Nothing is worth the pain you and I have suffered from…I was heartless." He hung his head in shame.

"Gary, two weeks ago you said the same thing. I wasn't home two days…two days was all it took for you to…" she choked back her tears. "I don't know if I can go back to a man that has cheated on me."

He looked up and held her eyes with his. "I never had sex with that woman; it was just a phone thing. I know I shouldn't have done it...but I can't change the past." He lifted a hand and caressed her cheek. "I can promise you, it will never happen again. I learned a valuable lesson...I love you and refuse to lose you. Please say you'll give me another chance."

His pleading eyes were more than she could stand. The knot in her stomach eased and her throat no longer burned. "Let's go in and have lunch." Gary's eyes brightened. "We can discuss this over food...one of your favorites, pizza." When she smiled, she watched the tension melt away from him. A sparkle entered his eye and the rose hue in his cheeks slowly bloomed. He immediately stepped out of the car and rushed to help her out.

As they approached the restaurant, Gary's demeanor began to liven. "I swear if you agree to come home...it won't be like two weeks ago, I'll make sure everything is clean. I'll fold the laundry and put it away. I'll make a great dinner for the three of us...God Tanya; you just have to agree to come home."

He rushed to the front door, pulled it open and waited for her to enter. She remembered before they were married he used to do the same thing, but over time, the chivalry died and he practically pushed her out of the way to be the first to enter a building. She smiled as she stepped past him, "Thank you Gary." She waited for him to enter. "It's been a long time since you held a door for me."

"Too long." He said as they approached the small welcoming podium. "It's been a long time for a lot of things, and I'm going to make it up to you." He smiled at the woman standing behind the desk. "Table for two please, oh...ah, and could you seat us near the back?"

The woman nodded and guided them to a booth near the back. The dining room was dimly lit; booths lined each side with a row of tables between. White table cloths covered the tops, and the decorative cast iron chairs added to the ambiance. Tanya climbed into the booth. The stiff vinyl squeaked as she slid to the center of the bench. Gary stood at the head of the wall mounted table while he waited for her to get comfortable. Sliding into the seat opposite hers, he grasped her hands and pressed them to his lips. He stared lovingly into her eyes. "Sweetheart, would you like a glass of wine?"

Tanya nervously picked at the heavy plastic encasing the menu. "No thanks, I have to drive. Besides if I have a glass of wine I'll get sleepy and won't be able to spend time with Jason later."

By the time the couple finished their pizza, Tanya had agreed to think about returning home. "I just want to be sure you're not just being nice to get me home. I think if we spend some time apart and kind of…ah, date, maybe we'll be able to work things out."

He smiled brightly, "That's all I'm asking. I just want to be able to prove to you the mean, disrespectful Gary is gone, and the new and improved version is sitting on the shelf waiting for you to take him home."

After paying the tab, Gary rushed to the front door and held it open. Tanya smiled as she passed by. "Wow I think I could get used to this."

He wrapped an arm around her, kissed her cheek and walked her to the car. He whispered, "I can honestly say, I have never loved anyone, as much as I love you."

Tanya pressed her back against her car. She smiled shyly while fidgeting with her keys. "When I came here today, I had no intention of sharing a meal with you let alone enjoying your company." She looked up and stared into his eyes. "I think I like the new improved Gary."

He stepped closer and placed his hands on her waist. "Can I kiss you?" He asked. Love sparked in his eyes. Tanya was taken aback. The shimmer of love in his eyes hasn't

been there since before they were married.
She nodded. He leaned in and kissed her lips
lovingly, tenderly, not like a man wanting to
consume a woman, more like a man who was
handling a cherished item. He lifted his head.
"When can I see you again?"

Tanya's knees felt like rubber. She was a
little breathless when she replied, "If you'd
like to come on Wednesday..."

"Perfect!" His face beamed. "Bring Jason
and we'll have a nice family dinner. Then we
can take him to that new movie he wanted to
see."

Surprised, Tanya's eyes widened and a
smile crossed her lips. "Really? You're willing
to go to the movies with us?"

"Really." He said as he yanked open her
door. "I've missed out on a lot of family
times. I want Jason to be able to look back
and remember his dad as a fun guy, not a
mean bastard. It's time I stepped up to the
plate and started being his daddy instead of
just his father."

Tanya kissed him and slid into the car.
After closing the door, Gary bent, kissed the
tips of two fingers and pressed them to the
glass. He mouthed, "I love you." She shifted
the car and headed to her mother's feeling a
whole lot better than she had in years.

Chapter 27

By the time Saturday, of that same week rolled around, Tanya and Gary were getting along great together. Although she was still with her parents, Tanya and Jason had spent the past few days with Gary. She decided they would return home and get on with their lives as a happy family.

Gary arrived just after ten Saturday morning to help them pack their things to return home. Gary and Bob stood on the patio waiting for Jason to join them. Gary was elated. "Bob, I can't express how happy I am to have my beautiful wife and son to finally come home. These past three weeks have taught me a harsh lesson. I never realized how precious a loving relationship is." He clapped Bob on the shoulder. "I promise, I'll never put Tanya through the heartbreak and pain she's suffered because of my wrong doings."

Bob scowled, "Let me tell you this Gary, if you break my daughter's heart again, I'm afraid it will take a lot more than sweet words to get her back." He raked his fingers through his salt and pepper hair. "You'll not only have her to deal with, but rest assured, I'll step in. There is no reason to treat anyone the way you've treated my daughter.

Gary hung his head in shame. "I know Mr. McBride, and I truly am ashamed of myself. Tanya's a good woman and a great mother…I'm blessed she took me back."

"I sincerely hope the feelings you have for my daughter…the feelings you're experiencing right now, stays with you for a very, very long time."

Jason interrupted the conversation. "Daddy, mommy needs your help."

Gary smiled down at his son. "Tell mommy I'll be right there."

Bob lifted Jason and walked to the patio doors. "I'm going to miss my little buddy."

Gary helped Jason into Tanya's car and secured the seatbelt. Charlie was sitting on the seat beside him. Gary scowled down at the raggedy teddy bear. "I think it's time to get a new teddy bear that one has seen better days."

Jason had a horrified look on his face. "I don't want a new teddy bear…I love Charlie."

"We'll talk about this when we get home." He scrubbed his hand over his son's head, straightened his back and closed the door.

Tanya approached the car and peered in at Jason. She noticed he was crying. "Gary." She said with concern in her tone. "What's wrong with Jason?"

"I don't know, maybe he's upset he's leaving."

She continued staring through the glass. "I'll find out when we get on the road." She wrapped her arms around Gary's waist, turned her eyes to his.

He bent his head and kissed her softly. "Let's get going. I'd like to stop for lunch at that pizza place...the one designed for kids."

She smiled brightly. "Jason will be so happy. That's his absolute favorite place to eat." She climbed into her car, and Gary slid into his after helping Tanya get settled. They backed out of the driveway. Gary followed her, feeling better than he had in weeks.

Tanya tried for ten minutes to get Jason to speak. "Sweetie, please tell mommy what's wrong." She glanced at him through the rearview mirror. Jason was holding Charlie tight. His face was buried in the crook of the bear's neck and he was sobbing. It broke her heart to see her son cry. "Sweetie, why are you crying?"

Jason lifted his head and wiped his tear stained with the back of his hand. He cried so hard he had a difficult time speaking through the quaking. "Da... Daddy....said he..." More tears fell and he sucked in a deep shuddering breath. "Daddy said its t...time...to g...get a new teddy bear he...s...said Charlie... has seen b...better days" He returned to his wailing.

Tanya was pissed. How dare Gary tell him he was getting him a new teddy bear? He should know by now, there could never be a replacement for Charlie. "Don't worry baby. I won't allow your father to take away Charlie."

Jason dried his eyes on Charlie's plush body he then dragged his forearm across his nose leaving a simmering streak of snot behind. "Do you promise?"

She wanted to cry. The pain her son was suffering through was uncalled for. What she really wanted to do was pull to the side of the road and let Gary see what he's done to his son. "I promise!" She clenched her teeth. Trying to relive the anger that was building inside her, she sucked in a deep breath and released it. "Nothing will happen to Charlie. I'll talk to your father as soon as we get home...will that be all right with you?"

Jason nodded. "Thank you mommy. Me and Charlie love you to the moon and back."

Tanya's heart strings tightened, "I love you too sweetheart."

Chapter 28

Tanya pulled into the driveway ahead of Gary. Although she had twenty minutes to calm down during the ride, she was still stewing. She wondered if he had been serious when he threatened to take Charlie away from Jason. She also wondered how he could just toss a child's beloved teddy bear into the trash. *What kind of person could do that?* She asked herself. *How can a father inflict so much unhealthy stress on his child?*

Deep in thought, she never noticed Gary's approach until she felt the door being pulled open. She stared up at the smiling face of her husband…Tanya's was not, as a matter of fact her face almost looked sour. "Gary, I think we need to talk."

He scowled. Thinking things were going to be better, Gary wondered why she looked and sounded aggravated. "Is there something wrong?"

"Not now, we'll talk in the house." She jerked her head toward the back seat.

"Oh…ah okay." He skirted the car and opened Jason's door. "Hey bud, let's go inside."

Jason slid out of the car dragging Charlie with him. His face was stained from dried tears. Walking as if he was on his death march, Jason wrapped his arms protectively around Charlie and held the bear tight.

Gary met Tanya at the rear of the car. "Why is he acting like someone stole his lollipop?"

"Maybe, someone tried to take away his happy." She replied snippily and walked away.

His eyebrows knitted together. "What is that supposed to mean?"

"Gary, he believes you're going to throw Charlie in the trash." She stopped, and turned on her heels to face him. "If you do that I swear…"

"Whoa, whoa…" He held his hands up in a halting motion. "I don't know what you're talking about….who the hell is Charlie?"

Tanya released a deep guttural growl and began to pace. "Jason is five years old! He got Charlie on his first birthday…from you no less!" She stopped pacing and glared up at him. "For your information…father of the year, Charlie is the name of the teddy bear he has been dragging around forever. I need you to stop threatening to throw his beloved bear in the trash." She covered her face with her hands to hide her tears.

"Tanya, I honestly didn't know that thing was so important to him." He wrapped his arms around her and pulled her close. "I promise, I'll never mention getting rid of it again." He kissed the top of her head. "I've heard him talk about Charlie, but I had no idea he was talking about that toy."

She dried her eyes with the heels of her hands. "Just don't say anything to him about it being a baby toy, or you're going to by a new bear to replace that one, and most of all please don't call it ratty or disgusting."

"I guess I should go apologize to him...Damn it, it seems like I can't do anything right."

They walked into the house and Gary set out to ease Jason's mind

Chapter 29

Three months later Tanya was getting Jason ready to go out trick or treating. Gary entered the house, slapped a pink slip on the table and growled, "I've been laid-off!"

Tanya was on her knees tying the back of Jason's Spiderman costume. She looked up and stared into Gary's raging eyes. "I'll just get a full time job. It's not that bad, we have a little money saved and…"

He slammed his hand down on the table causing her and Jason to jump. "What the fuck do you think you can do? You'll never make the amount of money I made…hell I wouldn't give you a dime for the shit you can do."

Tears welled in her eyes. "Gary, I don't think we should be discussing this right now."

"That's right spend time trick-or-treating…that's about all you're good for." He yanked open the refrigerator and pulled out a beer. He twisted the top off and with a snap of his finger he sent the cap sailing through the air hitting Tanya on the cheek. She growled. "Gary, why don't you grow up? Stop acting like the whole world is going to fall apart." She plucked the cap off the floor, rose to her feet and tossed it into the trash.

"There's no reason you have to toss shit around just because life threw you a curve. You'll get unemployment, I can find a better job...we'll be fine."

He scoffed. "Hell of a lot you know." He waved a hand toward the door. "Get away from me you worthless piece of shit...take Jason trick-or-treating and let him have a nice night away from here. I'm going to watch a little television to get my mind off shit."

By the time Tanya and Jason returned, Gary was in a fit of rage. "What the hell took so long? I thought you were going around the neighborhood not the entire fucking town!"

Jason's eyes welled with tears as Tanya guided him into the kitchen. Hearing growling in the background, she calmly explained, "Let's take off this costume and then you can take a bath."

With the innocence of a child Jason stared into his mother's eyes and asked, "Why does daddy always have to be mean? He always ruins my happy days."

"Oh sweetie, he's not taking anything out on you." She brushed the back of his head with her hand. "Daddy just has a hard time dealing with things that happen."

He dried his eyes with the sleeve of his costume. "Nothing happened the day we went to the fair...he yelled and we didn't even do anything wrong." He stepped out of the bright red and blue costume. "Yesterday when we had the macaroni the way grandma makes it, the stuff I love, he screamed and yelled something about eating slop." He stared in wide-eyed wonderment. "Is that slop mommy?"

She clenched her teeth. "No baby, it's not slop. Your father just didn't feel like eating the goulash. He wanted to eat what he always wants…meat and potatoes."

"Yeah but he said, 'nobody likes it.' I like it mommy, why did he say that when he knows I like it?"

"I like it too." Tanya sat him in a chair and untied Jason's shoes. "Who knows why he says the things he does."

"Sometimes I think daddy hates us."

Trying to hide the shock on her face, she stood up, turned toward the sink and caught a tear that began to roll. "Jason, your father doesn't hate you…" She didn't want to tell him she felt the exact same way. "He just…well he just wants things done his way. So when he yells while you're playing, or when you're watching television, it doesn't mean he hates you…it's just…he wants to watch television or peace and quiet."

Jason slid off the chair, picked up his shoes and started to walk out of the room. "Yeah, he turned off my favorite show so he could watch the music channel. Now I'll never know what happens to those dogs."

Tanya remembered that day. Jason was watching 'All Dogs go to Heaven' when Gary walked into the room, turned off the video player and shooed his son out of the room. "Oh Jason, maybe Santa will bring you the video for Christmas."

"Christmas is like a hundred years away. I'll forget what I already watched." He held one small hand on his hip.

"Well, you'll own it. You'll be able to watch it over and over as many times as you want."

His eyes brightened. "I can keep it? I won't have to take it back to the video place?"

Tanya laughed out loud. "Baby, you have all those videos in the cabinet. You know you don't have to take those back. Why would you think you would have to return a movie Santa gave you?"

"We always have to take back the good movies. The ones in the cabinet are old." They walked out of the kitchen and up the stairs. While getting his bath ready Tanya heard Jason murmur over the sound of the water pouring into the tub. "Bet he'll turn it off on me at the good part again...I'll never see the whole thing."

After turning off the water, and helping Jason get undressed, she helped him into the water and gave him his bucket of bath toys. Tiny boats floated among rubber ducks, and she watched as the little boy's sadness washed away. A smile crossed her gloomy face; she loved watching her son enjoy bath time.

After tucking Jason in and reading a story, Tanya walked solemnly out of his room. She hadn't realized how much her five year old son had been disturbed by the actions of his father.

Chapter 30

Tanya was getting Jason ready to go to Thanksgiving dinner at her parent's house, and he was so excited about having a turkey dinner. Ever since they've been married, Gary and Tanya rotate holidays between the two families. Last year they spent Thanksgiving with his family, so this year the holiday would be spent with Shelly and Bob. "I can't wait for the turkey." Jason said with excitement. "Grandma makes the best turkey dinner ever."

Gary sat on the sofa listening to his son's excitement. "If you want to call dried out turkey and over cooked vegetables a nice dinner, then you need to spend more time eating real food."

"Grandma makes real food." He said scowling. "Right mommy? Grandma's food is real?"

"Gary you have to get ready to go."

"Just a minute, this show's almost over."

She glanced at the television then looked at the digital display on the cable box. "We'll never make it if you don't get ready now."

"Shut the fuck up! I told you as soon as this show is over I'll get ready!"

Knowing they had a ninety minute drive, Tanya was getting upset. "Can you at least tell me what clothes you're going to wear, so I can press them for you?"

Gary gritted his teeth. He tossed the remote onto the coffee table and growled. "I can see I'm not going to be able to watch this without hearing your God damned mouth." He rose to his feet, climbed the stairs and entered the bathroom. Tanya stared up at the ceiling and wondered why he always waited until it was time to leave before he even started to get ready.

"Mommy, can Charlie come?"

Of course he can, we can't leave him home while we celebrate a holiday…" She turned to look at him. "Charlie's a part of the family. Go on upstairs and get him ready while I get the salad out of the fridge."

Once the salad bowl was in a tote, Tanya turned the iron on and waited for Gary to give her the clothes he needed pressed. She was reading the newspaper when she heard the gurgling water from the shower stop. After waiting a few minutes, she walked to the stairs and called up to her husband. "Gary, toss me down your clothes so I can press them."

"What the hell is your problem? I don't even know what I'm wearing yet."

She heard him rummaging around in their bedroom. Standing at the bottom of the stairs, she rested her elbow on the newel post.

Tanya was suddenly struck in the head with a pair of black jeans and a grey polo shirt.

"Why the hell didn't you tell me you were tossing these down?"

"Are you fucking stupid? You told me to throw them down, so I did. Now your bitching like you weren't expecting them."

"Actually I wasn't expecting them. You should have warned me."

She draped the garments over her left forearm and stepped into the kitchen. She pressed the shirt and hung it over the top of a chair and returned to her ironing. Bellowing came from the top of the stairs and Jason was crying.

Quickly she ran to the bottom of the stairs and noticed Gary was holding Charlie in his hand above Jason's head. "You are not taking this piece of shit in my truck! If you want to take a toy, take something you can play with."

Tanya rushed up the stairs and grasped Charlie's plush body. She glowered. "Give it to me."

Gary had a white towel tied around his waist. The water from his shower dripped from his hair and ran down his bare shoulder. He turned his blood shot eyes to stare into her's "He's not taking this piece of shit." He pulled the bear from her hand and carried it downstairs. "Believe me, as soon as he gives up this disgusting piece of shit, the better off

[170]

he'll be." He stood in the center of the large kitchen, his eyes scanned the room. "I thought you were pressing my clothes." He growled while waving Charlie in front of him.

"I was, but when I heard Jason crying I had to go see what was happening."

"I was there! I handled the situation." Tanya knew by the tone of his voice and the rage in his eyes, she had to be quiet or he'd lash out at her. "Get your ass moving! You've been bitching at me all morning...now you fucking stand there like you have nothing to do. Move your ass!"

Tanya scurried past him, stood in front of the ironing board and started pressing his jeans. She thought, *why do I have to press his clothes? I always have to get myself ready, get Jason dressed and pack everything we'll need for the day...I'm also responsible for pressing his clothes. All that asshole does is take a shower and bitch.*

Tanya was startled out of her train of thought when Gary slammed his hand down firmly on the ironing board. "What the hell's wrong with you? I told you last week I want a crease in my jeans..." He pulled the pants off the board and hung them on one finger by a belt loop. "Does this look like they have a crease?" He tossed the jeans hitting Tanya in the chest. "Can you make a crease? Is that tiny pinhead of a brain big enough to figure it out?"

Tears welled in her eyes. She lifted the jeans, and readied the legs to press a sharp crease down the center. As she started to press, Gary stood at the end of the ironing board shouting out orders. "I don't want the crease to be off to the side. Make sure you use spray starch on them so the crease will stay all day."

Tanya wanted to shove the iron on his face to see if his skin would crease, but she remained where she was, head bowed and not saying a word.

Once he finished dressing, Gary growled. "Get your ass and Jason's into the car."

Tanya grabbed Charlie from the table where Gary had tossed it and pressed it between her abdomen and forearm. She grasped the tote with the salad, slung Jason's backpack over her shoulder along with her purse, and grabbed Jason's hand. "Come on sweetheart." She said softly to Jason. "Let's get in the car before he starts yelling again."

She was just about to step through the front door when Gary grabbed the strap of Jason's backpack pulling her back into the house. "Jason go get in the car. Your mother and I will be out in a minute."

Tanya turned to face Gary. "What are you doing?"

"Give me that fucking piece of shit!" He yanked Charlie out of her arm. "I told him he wasn't taking this ratty toy…" He walked into the kitchen and tossed the bear into the trash. "That settles it. I suggest you get in the car so we can go eat the slop your mother has cooked."

Tanya wanted to slap him. She tried to rush to the trash but he pulled her back and shoved her toward the door. Tears streamed down her face and the pain she hadn't felt in her stomach in two months returned. Bile seeped into her throat. She needed her prescription but he insisted on blocking the path to the bathroom. She hung her head and cried as she stepped through the door.

Tanya closed Jason's door after checking his seatbelt, she reached her hand out to grasp her door handle, and was shocked when the car started moving. Quickly she flung the door open, and side stepped to keep from being knocked down by the open door. She literally had to leap into the car while Gary started backing out of the driveway faster. He laughed and shrugged. "You told me we were in a rush…what's the matter did you tire your fat ass out getting a little exercise?"

Tanya new she was a bit overweight, and he knew his comments always hurt her feelings. She hung her head and tears began to flow. She snapped her seatbelt into place. "Gary." She said while sliding Jason's backpack off her arm. "I really don't appreciate you degrading me in front of Jason."

[173]

"It's not my fault you're fat…maybe you should lose weight then people wouldn't make comments."

As he drove he continued to badger her about everything from her weight, to her clothes, to the salad she made. Finally she was fed up with his rude comments; she lifted her head and faced him. "I don't know what the hell crawled up your ass, but I'd appreciate it if you'd just leave me alone."

Jason said from the back seat. "Mommy where's Charlie?"

Tanya gritted her teeth and scowled at Gary. "I'm sorry honey, daddy left him home."

Loud wailing erupted from the back seat. "Now why did you have to go and tell him I left it home?"

"Well you did. You took it…"

"Shut the fuck up! You're such an asshole. Now I have to fix the situation…as usual." He peered into the rearview mirror and looked at his son. "Hey buddy, don't worry, Charlie's fine…he…ah…wanted to stay home to take a nap."

Jason dried his eyes with the back of his hands. "He's going to be scared."

"No, no, he's fine. You'll see as soon as we get home."

Tanya pursed her lips. "You know Gary; he's going to want to see Charlie as soon as we walk in the door…then what the hell will you do? Pull it out of the trash and hand it to him?" She turned to face her window and stared at the scenery passing by.

"It's not what I'm going to do; it's what you're going to do. You shouldn't have let me throw the piece of shit away in the first place.

She turned her head and glared at him. Her face was red and her stomach was killing her. She growled. "My fault...my fault! How could you possibly say, you throwing away Charlie was my fault?" She turned her face away and began to cry.

"If you think we're going to your mother's while you and Jason are crying, you're out of your fucking mind. I swear if you don't stop, I'll turn around and we can have leftovers for Thanksgiving dinner!" He glared at Jason in the mirror. "Between you and your pathetic mother...you have ruined another holiday!"

They arrived at the McBride home over an hour late. Bob stood in the driveway with a worried look on his face when Gary finally parked. Gary looked at his father in-law, turned and said softly, "Ready to go?" He pasted on a fake smile and pushed open the door.

All during dinner Gary poured on the sickening sweet charm. He complimented Sherry's cooking even though Tanya knew he was just trying to come across as a sweet loving man. Gary thought Tanya's parents were easily fooled, but they saw right through his phony façade. As soon as Tanya returned from the trip from hell, she fished Charlie out of the trash. After washing and drying the bear, she handed it to Jason. "Sweetie, Charlie's all clean and wants to know if you'd like him to sleep with you tonight."

Jason grabbed the bear, still warm from the dryer, and held him tight. He whispered, "I was so lonely without you." After placing a kiss on the top of the head, he looked up at his mother. "Why does daddy have to be so mean? He wouldn't let Charlie go with us, and he doesn't even eat much."

Tanya's heart was breaking. "I don't know sweetie, but maybe we should be extra nice to daddy because he's...ah, well he's sad because he lost something."

"Yeah, I get sad when I lose stuff too." He thought for a long moment. "But I don't get mean about it."

Tanya smiled. "That's enough about your father. Let's read a story so we can both relax and have a good night's sleep.

Chapter 31

It's been two weeks since the Thanksgiving mockery and Gary's mood hadn't changed. As a matter of fact Tanya believed his mood had been getting progressively worse. Gary handed her a credit card. "Go out and get Jason some nice gifts for Christmas. I don't want to see any of the garbage you usually buy. Maybe you should get one of those games systems…and a couple of games."

Tanya removed the card from his hand and slid it into her wallet. "Is the game system for you" Or should I pick up games Jason would enjoy?"

Gary was standing next to the table when she asked the question. He swept an arm across the tabletop. Everything went sailing through the air and crashed to the floor. Glasses shattered and beverages sprayed in every direction. "I told you to pick up the system for him!" He bellowed. "If I wanted a game system don't you think I know where the store is? I can't depend on you to do anything right. Just go get the shit while I pick Jason up from my mother's."

Tanya slung her purse on her shoulder and crossed her arms. "Is there anything else I should pick up while I'm out?"

He glared at her. His cold eyes looked as if they could see into her very soul. "Are you fucking stupid…oh wait, don't answer that. I already know the answer." He released a menacing laugh. "Maybe I should stop talking to you; your mentality is starting to rub off on me."

Tanya hung her head and started walking to the door. Gary continued with snide comments while she stepped away from him. By the time she reached the car, her stomach was in knots and her head ached. Her trembling hands had all they could do to slide the key into the ignition and start the car. After taking a few deep breaths, she glanced into the rearview mirror and dried her eyes. *I don't know what I've done to deserve this…*

Gary slammed his hand on the window and growled "I forgot to tell you, go to the toy store in the mall. They have a coupon for a great game I've been eyeing."

"Do you have the coupon?"

"What the fuck! Do I have to do everything? The piece of shit is probably still on the floor where you left it."

Not wanting to look into his eyes, she held her head down, turned off the engine and climbed out of the car. After entering the house, Tanya picked up the newspaper he swept onto the floor and thumbed through the store ads. When she found the coupon, she ripped it out and shoved it into the back pocket of her jeans.

She was just about to leave when Gary said, "Did you get the right coupon? I hate paying full price for shit if I don't have too." He held his hand out for the small scrap of paper. After handing it to him, Gary read the fine print. "Good it's still valid. Don't forget to use it." He handed it back and she returned it to her pocket. "Don't take all day, you'll need you to pick up Jason while I try out the system…wouldn't want the little guy to be disappointed on Christmas with a broken machine."

Tanya scowled. "I thought you were picking him up."

"Oh…ah, yeah, but I thought this would be a better plan."

She shrugged and returned to the car. *I wish that man would make up his mind. I swear he's going to drive me crazy.* She thought as she maneuvered her way through the busy holiday traffic.

After doing the shopping, Tanya dropped the parcels off. Gary met her at the door like a kid waiting for a gift. He grabbed the bags out of her hand. "Go get Jason. I'll need a couple hours to check out the system and package it back up."

Tanya was tired from fighting the crowds at the mall. "Do you really need two hours?"

"I'm sorry; did I say something that confused you?" He was scowling. "Two hours." He held up two fingers and glanced down at his watch. "It's five fifteen now, I don't want you home until after seven…do you know how to tell time?" He laughed as he walked into the house with the bags under his arms.

By the time Tanya returned from the short trip that should've taken no more than twenty minutes, she was ready to relax. After kicking off her shoes and placing them in the closet, she hung her jacket and helped Jason with his. "Mommy, is daddy home?"

She nodded. "Yes, but I think he may be resting. Why don't you pick out a movie we can watch?" She knew what Gary was doing; she also knew it would be hours before he emerged from the room.

As soon as they finished watching the movie, Tanya sent Jason to bed. She sat in the living room flipping through the channels when Gary entered the room. "What's for dinner?" He asked while grabbing the remote from her hand.

"Jason and I ate at your mother's. She sent a plate home for you…" She looked at his scowling face. "I can heat it up if you want." With the look he was giving her she knew he wasn't willing to slide the plate in the microwave.

"Whatever it is, I don't want it. Why don't you go cook me a burger on the grill? I'm not in the mood for much more than that."

She knitted her eyebrows. "Can't you just have something I can cook inside? It's too cold to be standing on the deck."

He glared down at her sending cold chills up her spine. "What, I'm not good enough to cook dinner for. I suggest you get off your fat ass and heat up the grill."

Tanya reluctantly rose to her feet, slid on her shoes and coat and walked outside to heat the grill. *What the hell does he think I am? I have spent my day, as usual, catering to his every whim.* She clicked the electronic igniter, but the gas didn't light. After a few more tries, Tanya entered the house and grabbed a pack of matches.

She was shivering when Gary entered the room. "Don't tell me, you haven't started the grill yet."

Tanya hung her head. "No the button doesn't work. You were supposed to fix it last week."

He took two long strides and stood mere inches from her. He bent his face down and sneered. "Maybe I could get a few things done around here if I didn't have to constantly chase after your ass." Spittle flew from his mouth and landed on her face. "I swear, you're dumber than a fucking flea." She turned toward the back door. He screamed loud enough to wake the neighbors. "Where the hell do you think you're going?"

Not willing to turn to face the lunatic, Tanya murmured, "I'm going to light the grill so I can cook your food." Her stomach knotted and bile threatened to enter her mouth.

"Why bother? I guess I'll just have to have the shit my mother sent over. Unlike you, she thinks about me." He pulled the plate from the refrigerator, after placing the dish into the microwave he slammed the door so hard the little metal clasp bent. "That's fucking great!" He growled as he flung open the basement door and ran down the stairs. After a few short moments he returned with a pair of pliers and began repairing the microwave's door while he grumbled. "You know Tanya; this is your fault. If you had just…"

Having enough of his ridicule for one day she turned to face him. "Look asshole, I don't know how you figure damaging the microwave was my fault, you're the one who decided to take your aggravation out on it…I had nothing to do with it!"

Gary was stunned. He couldn't believe she was trying to blame him for the damage. He straightened his back and stepped toward her. In a voice that was to calm for the look in his eyes he said, "Of course it's your fault." She bit her lip as she listened to his explanation. "If you had just been able to do what you were supposed to do, this would've never happened. So tell me, how this isn't your fault."

Tanya cowered as he menacingly stood in front of her. She murmured. "Sorry if the things I do around here are…"

Gary lost it. He stepped forward forcing her to back away. When Tanya's back hit the counter, he pressed his body against hers, pinning her in place. With arms stretched out to the side, and pliers in hand, he growled. "The things you do…the things you do!" spittle sprayed her face and she wanted to gag. "Let me give you a little tip. You do nothing around here. You're a worthless piece of shit. I asked you to make me a hamburger and you couldn't even do that. Now the fucking microwave is broken…all because you!"

Pain shot through Tanya's stomach. Tears rolled down her cheeks mixing with Gary's spittle. Tanya fisted her hands to stop them from trembling while she listened to the uncontrollable rambling going on in front of her. Fear ran rampant through her body. All she could think about was getting away from him. Her thoughts jumbled his words. She couldn't understand a thing he was saying.

Finally after what felt like hours, Gary shoved himself away from her and returned to his task. Tanya dried her face with a paper towel and walked out of the room. The last thing she heard as she climbed the stairs was, "That's right you worthless piece of shit, go upstairs…just leave be down here to fix my own food! You're worthless! Cry bitch, it still won't change what you've done!"

Tanya closed the toilet lid and sat down. After pulling a towel from the closet, she pressed it to her face and sobbed. A few long moments later, she rose to her feet, turned on the shower, undressed and stepped inside.

Chapter 32

Christmas Eve was always a big deal for Gary's family. They had the traditional Italian dinner consisting of various types of fish, antipasto and pasta. Tanya knew whenever the family gathered together there would always be one voice trying to speak above all the others. In reality she knew dinner was nothing more than a lot of food and shouting.

After Gary and Tanya packed the car for the usual twenty mile trip to his grandmother's they entered the house. He pulled her into his arms and kissed her tenderly. Tanya's body tensed when she felt him wrap his arms around her. She had been married to him just over six years and the psychological damage he had inflicted upon her was taking its toll. She knew his good mood would only last until something didn't go according to his plan. He released her and she walked outside to finish packing the car.

Standing beside the vehicle, Tanya watched as Jason ran toward her with a tin full of cookies. In his excitement he slid, tripped and dropped the tin. Cookies smashed to the ground. Jason had crumbs all over him. His little chin quivered and tears began to flow.

Tanya rushed to her son, helped him to his feet and brushed bits of cookie from his hair. "Jason, are you alright?" She said as she examined his hands. "Does anything hurt?"

Staring down at the crumbled mess in the driveway he sobbed louder. Through his tears he said with panic in his voice, "Now daddy's going to yell at you...." He brushed his tears away with the sleeve of his coat.

"Don't worry about your father, it was an accident...it's no one's fault." She kissed his tear stained face. "Now go get in the car while I clean this mess." He walked past her. "Oh Jason, there's a box of tissues in the console, please blow your nose and dry your eyes."

"I will mommy." He said as he yanked open the rear passenger door.

Tanya had just finished cleaning the cookie mess when Gary walked out of the house. Scowling down at the empty tin in her hand he growled. "What the hell happened?"

Tanya looked at the tin, and dumped the few tiny crumbs on the driveway. "Oh...ah Jason tripped."

"I thought I told you to carry the cookies. Now because of your irresponsibility all those cookies have gone to waste...so fucking typical."

Tanya approached the steps but Gary halted her. "Where the hell do you think you're going?"

"Inside to get another tin of cookies…is that a problem?"

Gary glared at her. "Your entire life is my problem. You'd better move that fat ass if you're planning on going with us." He laughed menacingly as Tanya hurried past him. By the time she ran into the house, placed the empty tin in the sink, grabbed another tin and ran out of the house…Gary was gone. She stood on the stoop knowing he'd return, laughing as if he had played the best practical joke ever devised.

Ten minutes he made her stand in the cold. With every passing minute, Tanya wanted to go into the house and forget about his families festivities. If it hadn't been for Jason she would have.

Gary parked at the curb, pushed down the window and called out to her. "Come on we don't have all night!"

Tanya rolled her eyes, walked down the driveway and stood beside a rather large snow bank. Gary had parked so close to the curb there was no way for her to get in without climbing the snow and risking injury on the ice coated mound. She stood stalk still not willing to feed his demented mind. So many times his childish play has caused her injury and she refused to budge.

She heard the crunching of ice as it shattered under the pressure of the tires as Gary slowly backed up. When she was able to finally climb into the car and get situated, Gary growled, "What the hell is your problem?"

She sat in silence refusing to be dragged into another argument. He drove the short distance to the highway all the while trying to engage her into a conversation. Finally fed up with his voice she yelled. "Just shut-up! I'm tired of you treating me like I'm some worthless piece of crap. I swear if it wasn't for Jason I wouldn't be going to this family function of yours." She turned her head and stared out the window.

Gary complained about everything from her stupidity to her cooking skills. He called her a pea brain, worthless and ridiculed her mothering skills. As he turned onto the road leading to his grandmother's house he growled out an order. "Tanya I suggest you put on a happy face before we get there. If you think for one minute I'll stop when you have that look on your face…you're sadly mistaken." He stared into the rearview mirror while saying, "Jason, if you fucking embarrass me here, you'll have hell to pay."

Tanya glared at him. "Maybe if you were a bit nicer we wouldn't have these so called looks on our faces."

Gary slammed his fist down on the steering wheel causing the horn to sound. "I don't know why you think I'm always mean. I swear, you and Jason have the same mentality.

He has an excuse, he's five, you're twenty-six…grow the fuck up!"

Gary spied his father as soon as he turned into the driveway. After parking and sliding the keys into his pocket, he leapt out of the car and ran to Tanya's door. He yanked the door open, and held out his hand to help her to her feet. His father smiled as he watched his son being a complete gentleman.

Gary's father, John, wrapped Tanya in his arms and gave her a gentle kiss on the cheek. "It's so nice to see my favorite daughter in-law. How have you been?" Tanya was his only daughter in-law, but she graciously accepted his kind words.

She watched as Gary helped Jason out of the car. "I've been fine…did Jason tell you he's going on a field trip to the museum as soon as they get back from winter break?"

Gary scoffed, and his father glared at him. "What's wrong with Jason going to the museum?"

"Nothing's wrong…I was clearing my throat."

Tanya raised an eyebrow knowing Gary could care less about his son's school trips. "Why don't you and Jason go in…it's freezing out here. I'll help Gary with this stuff." John said when he noticed Tanya was shivering.

"Go on inside dad, I can get this. There's no sense in having all of us freeze."

As soon as Tanya stepped into the house, the aroma of pasta sauce entered her nose. She also recognized the scent of baked stuffed shrimp.

Gary's grandmother was standing in front of the stove with a pair of tongs in her hand. The sound of fish sizzling in frying pan entered her ears at the same time the older woman spoke. "Tanya." Grandma said with a smile. She placed the utensil on a prepared platter beside the stove. Stretching her arms out, she welcomed Tanya into her loving embrace. After giving Tanya a kiss on the cheek she said, "I hope you're hungry. I made some of your favorite dishes."

Jason and John entered the house. John pulled off Jason's coat and hung it in the closet. Tanya smiled when she heard the excitement in her son's voice.

Tanya glanced at the older woman. "I love all the dishes you cook …ah, that is except for the eel." She curled one side of her lip up. "I can honestly say, I can go the rest of my life without tasting that again."

A heavy rap on the door caused everyone to turn. Gary's arms were loaded with gifts and bags. Quickly John rushed to the door and swung it open. "Why didn't you tell me you needed help? When I asked, you said you could handle it" John said as he grasped a large bag of gifts.

Gary glared at Tanya. "I thought my wife would've offered to help. I should've known I couldn't depend on her."

Tanya was very close to tears when John stepped in to defend her. "Gary your wife has enough to do. She was taking care of Jason and greeting your grandmother. If you needed help, it was your responsibility to ask...or at the very least make two trips."

"Look dad, I'm tired of everyone thinking my wife is great. If you'd like to know the truth about her...give me a week and I'll tell you everything."

Tanya's eyes welled with tears. She had always tried to do everything Gary asked, but he was always so ungrateful. "Gary, why do you always have to be so mean?"

"Mean?" Gary walked past her with his burdens in his arms. "You have no idea what mean is. I'm the nicest guy you know." He bumped into the table and the tin of cookies went flying. The cover flew off and the cookies scattered across the floor. "What the fuck!' He bellowed as he placed the remainder of the items on the table. "You are nothing but a worthless bitch."

John grabbed the broom from the closet and started sweeping the cookies into a pile. He glared at Gary. "Stop talking about your wife like that!" He demanded as he swept the cookies into the dustpan. "Why do you always have to blame others for the things you do?

It's not Tanya's fault you dropped the cookies."

"Yes it is if she had carried the piece of shit in, they wouldn't have spilled. Face it dad, my wife is worthless."

John noticed tears trickling down Tanya's face. He wrapped an arm around her and guided her to the living room. "Have a seat. I'll go straighten out his attitude."

Tanya sat on the stiff sofa, wrapped her arms around herself and hung her head. "Please don't say anything that will get him going. I've already heard how worthless I am…I just don't want to hear arguing. It's Christmas Eve; I would've thought he could at least respect you and grandma. I probably should've stayed home."

"Nonsense! Gary will be fine once we start eating. I'm sure whatever's going on in his head will go away once he relaxes."

Tanya shrugged. "Please just drop it, I know him and I have to live with his attitude…please don't make it any harder on me."

John sat in the chair across from her. He rested his elbows on his knees and laced his fingers. "I know he has a hot temper, I also know he doesn't mean half the things he says. Just let me talk to him…I promise, if he starts to holler, I'll kick him out. None of us needs to be aggravated on a holiday."

Tanya didn't say a word. She just sat on the sofa knowing John was going to do things his way. She had witnessed the arguments between father and son, and they always made her stomach tense.

John rose to his feet and walked out of the room. A few brief moments past before Tanya heard the two men arguing. Jason ran into the room and snuggled close to his mother. He whispered, "Why are daddy and grandpa yelling?"

Tanya glanced down at her son. "Grandpa's just trying to calm your father down. Don't worry." She held him close while they listened to Gary belittle his father.

Fifteen minutes later Gary stormed into the room, and growled. "Get your shit we're leaving!"

Jason started to cry. "I don't want to go."

"I didn't fucking ask you if you wanted to go…I'm telling you to get your shit, put your coat on and get into the car." Jason reluctantly slid off the sofa and ran to gather his things.

Tanya remained seated. Her face was red and tears began to trickle down her cheeks. A tear rolled onto her lips and she licked the acrid liquid away with the tip of her tongue. She dried her face with the back of her hands. "Why can't you just calm down. Why do you have to ruin the holiday for Jason. He's been looking forward to this night for weeks."

Gary scoffed, "Maybe you should've thought about that, before you made me carry in all the shit." He stood in the doorway and slammed his hands into the trim causing a loud slapping sound. Tanya glared up at him as he continued his ranting. "Get off your fat ass and get into the car. I refuse to eat a meal with people who disrespect me."

Tanya rose to her feet. "So you're going to ruin Jason's holiday, because you can't act like a normal human…is that it?"

He took two quick strides, stood directly in front of her leaned down close to her ear and said in a tone so low only Tanya could hear "Maybe you like it when your husband is treated like shit. I think you should get into the car and shut your fucking mouth. From now on if you don't have anything intelligent to say…keep your fucking mouth shut." He stepped back and held his arm out toward the door. "Go; tell Jason we're leaving right now.

By the time Tanya entered the kitchen; Jason had his coat on and was standing beside the door. Tanya said while sliding her coat on, "I'm sorry we have to leave."

John stepped forward and said softly, "If you need anything give me a call. I'll stop by tomorrow morning to give Jason his gifts. Please don't be upset, we all know how he gets."

Tanya opened the door and led Jason to the car. Fifteen minutes past before Gary finally walked out the door. He wasn't wearing his coat. He pulled her door open, leaned down and said in a calm tone. "Come on in, I think we should stay to celebrate with Grandma."

Tanya eyed him suspiciously. "So everything is alright now? What changed your mind?"

"Never mind, just help Jason out and I'll meet you inside." He leaned in close and kissed her lips. While staring into her eyes he said, "I love you." He ran his thumb down the side of her face. He held his hand out. "Come on, let me help you." Tanya placed her hand in his and he pulled her to her feet. He wrapped his arms around her and whispered, "I'm sorry I acted like an ass. I don't know what gets into me sometimes."

The remainder of the evening went by without further argument. While Gary drove home he apologized for the way he treated Tanya and Jason. He also said he would make it a point to change his attitude. Tanya never found out the reason behind his change of heart, she was just happy Jason had the opportunity to spend Christmas Eve with his grandfather.

Chapter 33

It's been seven years since Tanya married Gary. Her entire life had been flipped upside down. The once vibrant young woman wallows in her disgrace. Reminiscing over her past, Tanya sat at the kitchen table, a tear rolled down her cheek. She wondered how she could've allowed her life to fall into hell's pit of depression and disrespect. The life she lived was full of torment, ridicule and judgment. Although the ties that bound Tanya to her marriage were invisible, they held her stronger than any steel chains ever could.

Gary was a controlling manipulative man who dragged his 'loving wife' into the dirt on a daily basis. He shoveled the soil of shame and injustice over her fragile ego whenever he had the chance. He cared little about her feelings, and wasn't ashamed to embarrass her wherever he felt it would cause the hardest impact.

He entered the kitchen with the usual scowl on his face. He eyed Tanya and noticed she was crying. "What the hell's wrong with you?"

She dried her tears, stared down at the table and lied. "Nothing, I was just thinking about a book I read."

Gary scoffed. "The so called books you read are nothing but garbage. I have a good mind to through the shit away."

She glanced up from the table and into his spiteful eyes. "Why would you do that?"

He shrugged. "Because I can. If they have nothing to offer, no knowledge to share, they're as worthless and the pile of shit that reads them."

Tanya rose to her feet and walked to the counter. Her hands trembled when she reached for a glass. "Why do you always have to make me feel like shit…whenever I enjoy something you always tell me it's no good…no matter what it is….why?"

"Most of the shit…No let me restate that, all of the shit you like is worthless. You sit in the living room every night doing that thing with the ropes…"

"It's call macramé."

"Alright, macra-fucking-me…it's worthless. Why don't you do something creative?"

Tanya turned to face him. She knitted her brows and braced herself for an argument. "What the hell do you call macramé? It's creative, and as I recall you enjoy the huge hanging table on the porch. As a matter of fact, you were the one who told me to make it."

He took two long strides and sneered into her face. "I have a good mind to go in there…" He jerked an arm toward the living room door. "…and throw all that worthless bullshit away!" He stormed out of the kitchen and toward the living room.

Tanya could hear him tossing things around in the living room, and tears spilled from her eyes. She wanted to go into the room, but she wasn't sure if he'd hit her with a flying object. She knew he was in there destroying her things. She also knew he would enter the kitchen, in a few minutes, with a smug look on his face and tell her to go clean the mess she made him create.

As his temper raged on, she sat at the table and covered her ears. She could hear his bellowing through her hands. "This fucking shit is worthless….I can't believe how anyone could possibly enjoy playing with fucking string."

As soon as he left the living room, he walked through the front door and onto the three season porch. Tanya rose to her feet and approached the doorway. She watched as he yanked the hanging table from ceiling, hook and all. She heard the shatter when he tossed the thick piece of glass onto the asphalt driveway. Tears flowed freely down her face while she continued to watch his hideous display from the open doorway.

His breath sawed in and out as he slowly calmed. His face was red, and his eyes were blood shot by the time the raging fit came to an end.

He pushed past Tanya, nearly knocking her to the floor. "Clean the shit up. Clean the driveway first; I don't want the neighbors thinking we're a bunch of pigs.

Tanya stood in stunned silence while she listened to her husband bark out orders. Finally, after a few long arduous minutes, Gary's mouth became silent. She let out a huge sigh of relief and started cleaning.

She entered the kitchen to grab the broom; Tanya noticed Gary sitting at the table reading the newspaper. He glowered at her as she passed his chair; giving her the feeling she was doing something unacceptable to him. His cold dark eyes watched her every move. She opened the closet door and pulled out the broom.

She could feel Gary's stare on her as she started to walk across the room. She was nearly past him when she felt him firmly grasp the handle of the broom. He scoffed. "What the hell do you think you're going to do with this?"

She tried to yank the broom from his grasp. "I'm going to clean the driveway." She said without meeting his eyes. "That's what you wanted…right?"

He pulled the broom out of her hand and growled, "Are you a fucking idiot? Use the broom downstairs. This piece of shit is worthless." He tossed it on the floor.

Tanya picked it up and returned the broom to the closet. Leaving Gary alone, she descended the stairs and grabbed the push broom. She then opened the bilco doors leading to the backyard. Tanya refused to cross Gary's path until he calmed down.

Once the glass had been cleaned, she returned the broom back to its original location in the basement. She entered the house, walked into the kitchen and grabbed the trash container. Her throat was dry, but she knew if she stopped to get a drink Gary would make some snide comment and she was done hearing his voice for the day.

She entered the living room and was stunned when she saw the mess Gary had created with her macramé cord. There was rope of various colors and thicknesses tangled together. She knew there was little hope of separating the knotted mess, so she gathered up the pile of cord and tossed it into the trash.

Gary sat on the sofa watching television while she picked up the mess he had created. She glanced at him out of the corner of her eyes. She waited for him to say something mean and spiteful. He said, "Don't expect to go out and buy more of that shit." She replied under her breath, *don't worry I won't...I was working on a plant hanger your mother wanted, but now she can go to the store and purchase one. You can tell her why I can't make her one.*

By the time she finished cleaning the mess Gary created, all that remained was a few metal rings and decorative beads. She scowled down at the empty basket. A tear welled in her eyes, but she refused to allow Gary the satisfaction knowing he made her cry.

Chapter 34

Mother's Day of the same year was like every other holiday. It was always, Tanya and Jason would end up crying from the torment Gary put them through. Why would she think Mother's Day would be any different?

Gary planned for the family to spend the holiday with his mother. Although Tanya and Barbara started off on the wrong foot, Barbara respected Tanya for the tolerance and patience she had, dealing with Gary's temper.

Tanya was getting Jason ready for the Mother's Day dinner when Gary flew down the stairs and tossed a pair of black jeans and a white polo shirt at Tanya. "Do you mind pressing these while I take a shower?" His tone was unusually nice considering they only had fifteen minutes before they had to leave.

"Sure, do you want me to use spray starch on your shirt?"

"Whatever, just make sure the creases in the jeans are down the center…I like them nice and sharp. Make sure you spray both sides with the starch so the creases stay in even after I sit down. There is nothing worse than having only half the leg with a crease."

Tanya was taken aback; he was actually talking to her like a regular human. She set up the ironing board and proceeded to press Gary's clothes paying close attention to the creases in the legs and sleeves. She finished pressing the two items, put the iron and the board away and carried the garments up stairs and hung them neatly on hangers. She placed the hangers on a hook inside the bathroom door and said, "Your clothes are all set. I hung them on the door so you can get dressed as soon as you finish your shower."

Tanya walked downstairs and gathered the things they needed to take with them. Jason was in the living room watching television when Tanya heard the spray of the shower stop. Carrying a bag of gifts and a bouquet of flowers, Tanya walked out the door and placed the items in the trunk of the car.

As she approached the front door she heard Gary bellowing orders. After rushing through the door, she noticed Jason was crying. Tanya glared at Gary. "What the hell happened?"

"I told him to turn off the television but he refused. So he's punished. I don't want him watching television for two weeks."

"Two weeks? How many times did you tell him to turn it off?"

"It doesn't matter…he disobeyed me now he has to pay."

Tanya glanced down at her son. "Did your father tell you to turn the program off?"

Jason sucked in a deep shuddering breath and explained through his sobs. "Daddy walked into the living room and told me to change the channel...he wanted to watch the news. I didn't even have time to pick up the remote before he started yelling at me." Tanya handed him a tissue to dry his tears. "Why am I punished? I was doing it."

Tanya scowled at Gary. "Is he telling the truth?"

"What the hell difference does it make? I told him to do something and he blatantly ignored me. He's punished and that's final!" He tossed his hands in the air, sat on the sofa and slid into his shoes.

Tanya walked into the kitchen to finish packing the few remaining items they had to take. Suddenly Gary stormed into the kitchen, stood in front of her and bellowed to the top of his lungs. "I thought I told you to spray these pants. Did you fucking use the spray I bought or did you use the garbage you purchased last week?"

Tanya looked down at the jeans and she could clearly see the perfect crease running down the center of each leg. "What's wrong with them?" She knitted her brows while staring at the pants with confusion of her face. "There's a perfect crease in your pants...and for your information I did use the spray starch you bought."

"You couldn't have…the fucking shit is shiny. How the hell do you expect me to go to dinner with a line of shiny shit going down the length of my pants?" Gary slammed his fist down on the table causing Tanya to step back. "You are a fucking worthless piece of shit! Now I have to find another pair of jeans and press them myself because your fucking pea brain can't handle the simple task of pressing clothes."

He stormed out of the room and up the stairs. Tanya's entire body was trembling. She couldn't for the life of her figure out what the hell caused Gary to fly off the wall. The crease in his jeans was perfect, there was no shiny residue he mentioned, and he caused Jason to cry…all in less than ten minutes. Tears trickled down Tanya's cheeks when she placed the last item in a large paper bag. Relieved she had finished packing the bags; she walked to the foyer and placed them on the small table to grab on their way out the door.

Gary continued his ranting while he slammed doors and drawers in search of a new outfit. The raging fit lasted fifteen minutes. Finally he descended the stairs with a pair of blue jeans and a dark blue polo shirt draped over his arm. Tanya was sitting on the sofa with Jason beside her when Gary stood in the doorway glaring at her. "Did you set up the ironing board?" He growled. "Or was that too much to expect for your tiny brain to figure out?"

Tanya rose to her feet and walked into the kitchen to set up ironing board and iron. Once the iron was heating she entered the living room and softly said, "It's all set."

He glared at her as she sat in the overstuffed chair across from him. "As usual I have to do everything in this house." He growled as he walked out of the room.

Tanya looked at Jason. He was sitting in the corner of the sofa curled into a ball with his forehead pressed against his knees. She could hear him softly sobbing. After a few brief moments, she rose to her feet and stepped toward the sofa. Sitting beside her son, she rubbed his back while she whispered, "Don't worry, once we get to grandma's he'll be fine." Tears began to trickle down her cheeks. It broke her heart to see her son cry. She embraced him and kissed his cheek. "Tomorrow when your father goes to work, we'll go to the park and I'll push you on the swings. Just try to relax...please, for mommy."

Jason lifted his head and stared into her tear filled eyes. "I wish daddy was nicer to us."

"Me too baby...me too." She kissed his head and waited in silence for Gary to finish getting ready.

They were twenty minutes late getting on the road. Gary remained a force to be reckoned with, and his bad mood was wearing thin on Tanya's nerves. Trembling in the seat beside him, she had to listen to everything he hated about her including, her inability function as a normal human being. In the time it took to drive across town, he had succeeded in making her feel like the most worthless person on the planet. Tears ran down her face while she silently cried. Tanya stared out the window to avoid looking at him at all costs.

As they entered the house, the smell of pasta sauce and roasted lamb filled the air. Jason ran ahead and was in the process of hugging his grandmother when Gary's mouth erupted again. Barbara stood stock still in the center of the living room when she spied Gary entering the room. She looked past him and at the sorrowful face of her daughter in-law. Scowling she said, "What the hell did you do to Tanya?"

"I didn't do shit…what has she been telling you?"

Barbara held out her hand gesturing for Gary to take a look at his wife. "Look at her…she's been crying. Why is she crying if you didn't do anything?"

Tanya placed the parcels on the table and entered the living room. "I'm all right; I was just having a hard morning."

Gary turned and glared at her. "Did someone say something to you, because I don't remember anyone asking if Tanya was alright?"

Tanya hung her head, turned and stepped into the kitchen…away from Gary's cold stare. She returned to the living room when she heard Gary bellowing to the top of his lungs. "You're fucking worthless too, if you're going to take her side and not your son's. What the hell does it take for you to respect me for the man I am?"

Barbara's face turned red and her eyes were as cold as his. She growled. "Get out of my house." She pointed toward the front door. "I will not stand here and allow you to ridicule me! I don't want you coming back until you can apologize for the way you treated me…GET OUT!"

Gary picked up a chair and threw it with all his might at his mother. He sneered. "It will be a fucking cold day in hell before me or my family steps foot in this house again. I refuse to apologize. You're standing here accusing me of mistreating my wife…you're a fucking bitch!" He grabbed Jason and hauled him out of the house while he bellowed, "Tanya get your ass in the car."

Tanya stepped past Barbara. "I'm so sorry he treated you like that." She hung her head and walked out the door.

Realization of losing her grandchild popped into her head as soon as Tanya heard the door snap shut. Before she could make it to the car she heard Barbara's tear filled pleas. "Gary, please don't be like that. Please come back and have dinner…Please don't leave."

Gary paused beside the car. "You will never see your grandson…I refuse to allow him to socialize with a person like you."

Tanya helped Jason into the car. He was sobbing loudly and pleading with Tanya to make Gary stop. Tears flowed down her face. She had no idea how to rectify the situation. All she knew, Gary had snapped and she feared he would become physically abusive."

During the short ride home the car was filled with the sounds of Jason and Tanya silent sobs. Gary sat in the driver's seat with a smug look on his face. He parked in the driveway, turned to Tanya and said, "I'm sorry you had to see my mother act the way she did. I honestly have no idea why she snapped the way she did."

Tanya couldn't believe her ears. It wasn't Barbara who snapped, it was Gary. She knew right then and there, Gary had some serious mental issues and she knew he would never seek out medical treatment. Tanya reached for the door release and shoved the door open. "I think after everyone calms down you should give her a call."

"I won't be calling her. She disrespected me and my family…she can rot in hell for all I care." Tanya climbed out of the car, helped Jason to his feet and walked into the house leaving Gary alone with his thoughts.

It took more than six months for Gary to listen to what his mother had to say. It wasn't until Barbara apologized to Gary when he finally allowed Jason to visit with his grandmother.

Chapter 35

During the summer of her seventh year of marriage, Gary was going to school part time and he worked part time. Tanya reluctantly had to change jobs to work around his schedule, so Jason could have one parent with him at all time.

Tanya worked second shift in a large company assembling, and testing small tape cartridges used for various warheads. There were only three people working the nightshift, one was a male security guard who just so happened to take a liking to Tanya.

Every night Thomas would walk the halls of the huge building and stop to chat with Tanya during his rounds. Thomas was a tall muscular man whose green eyes were absolutely dreamy. His blonde hair was always neatly trimmed. Although he had to wear the drab guard's uniform, he always looked great.

Tanya was rushing out of the ladies room on her way back to her department, when she ran head on into Thomas. "Oh sorry Tom, I didn't mean to bash into you like that." She was drying her hands on a brown paper towel.

He wrapped his arms around her waist to keep her from falling, and chuckled. "I guess I should make sure I make my rounds whenever you're in the restroom." He winked. "I could get used to you falling into my arms."

Tanya was always timid around men, and Thomas was no exception. She shyly stepped away from him; with her head bowed she said softly, "I'll have to pay closer attention..." She rushed away. "I'm so sorry. It won't happen again."

Tanya was aggravated with herself. She couldn't believe she ran into the man who had been flirting with her, since the day she started second shift. He made it abundantly clear he wanted her to cheat on her husband. Sitting at her test station, with the department window to her back, she heard a soft tap on the glass. She didn't want to turn around, knowing Thomas was waiting for her to leave the department to talk with him. She silently hoped he'd go away. To Tanya's dismay the tapping continued. She rose to her feet and walked to the door.

"Tom, I'm really busy. I don't have time to talk to you right now."

"Well we both get off at midnight. Why don't you and I go for a quick drink?"

"I've told you before, I can't go anywhere. I have to be home at a certain time or Gary will go ape shit."

"Why don't you get rid of that guy? I can tell he doesn't respect you."

"Oh yeah, how can you tell that?"

Thomas leaned against the wall, and stared into Tanya's eyes. "I can tell just by the way you act whenever you talk about him…" He watched her face when he asked, "Does he hit you?"

Tanya scoffed. "No. Why would you think he hits me? As a matter of fact, I told him when we first got married, if he laid a hand on me, I'd kill him in his sleep."

Thomas pushed himself away from the wall. "Well if he does anything to hurt you, I swear, I'll personally kick his ass."

Tanya turned to walk back into the room. "Don't worry; he's just got a hot temper."

As she entered the room she heard Thomas say, "Let me know if you ever need a man to lean on." Tanya rolled her eyes and closed the door.

She was dead on her feet when she got out of work. Tanya walked across the dark parking lot with her keys in hand, and her purse slung over her shoulder. Spying a figure standing beside her car, she halted in her tracks. Her heart raced and her hands began to tremble. Slowly she approached the car with her keys fisted in her hand the longest key was strategically placed between her fore and middle fingers.

Thomas stood beside her car. "Hey Tanya, I was hoping you changed your mind."

Her racing heart slowed once she realized who was standing beside her car. After releasing the breath she was holding, she said, "Tom, I already told you, I can't go for a drink with you."

"I thought you were only saying that so your coworker wouldn't find out and tell your husband."

Tanya nudged him away from her car and unlocked the door. "No Tom, I really do have to get home." A knot formed in the pit of her stomach. "I don't want Gary going crazy in the middle of the night. My son has school in the morning and he needs his sleep."

He stepped away from her vehicle and held the door while she climbed in. "Well maybe some other time." Before he closed the door he said in a soft tender voice, "If you need someone to talk to, I want you to call me." He handed her a slip of paper with his phone number on it.

After removing the paper from his hand, Tanya absentmindedly placed it on the console and gave him a slight nod. She started the car and drove away.

As she closed the gap between work and home, Tanya's stomach knotted and cramped. She glanced down at the digital display and realized if she continued driving at the pace she was, she would surely be late. After pressing a bit harder on the gas, she wondered what would happen if she was ever in an accident or was stopped by police. Gary always waited up for her and she knew, sure as hell, she was going to have to hear his mouth. After turning into the driveway, she quickly leapt from the car and ran to the front door. Tanya was breathless when she walked through the front door.

Gary stood in the doorway preventing her from entering the kitchen. His elbows were braced on each side of the frame and his fingertips were resting on the head of the frame. He didn't smile, he didn't sneer, as a matter of fact; he showed no emotion at all. Tanya tossed her keys on the table beside the door, stepped forward, closed and locked the door.

Not daring to say anything, afraid of his mood, she decided she would wait until he spoke. As she approached the kitchen Gary stepped back granting her access. Being dead tired, all she wanted to do was, get a glass of water and go to bed. After pulling the refrigerator door open she heard Gary say, "What are you making for dinner?" His voice was calm and to Tanya's surprise, he actually sounded like he might have been in a good mood.

She turned to face him. "I wasn't planning on making anything. All I want to do is sit down and relax for a few minutes before I go to bed." She finally glanced into his eyes and she was sorry.

Gary blocked her path, his chest was extended as if on display, and his eyes were cold. "I'm hungry." Was the only thing he said.

The last thing Tanya wanted was an argument, but it appeared to her, Gary was in the mood to battle. So instead of relaxing, Tanya knew she was going to have to cook him something, or she'd never be able to go to bed. "What would you like me too cook for you?"

Gary bit his bottom lip while he thought. "Why don't you go to the store and buy a couple of steaks...oh and fries."

"You couldn't call me at work so I could've gone shopping during my lunch?"

He shrugged. "I wasn't hungry then."

Tanya eyed him suspiciously. "What the hell did Jason have for dinner?"

"I took him to McDonald's he had a happy meal while I had one of those new burgers...is that a problem?"

Tanya knew he just wanted to aggravate her and force her to cook something he probably wasn't going to eat. As a matter of fact, she knew he would be asleep on the sofa, with the television remote in his hand, by the time she returned home. "Can't you wait until tomorrow? I'm extremely tired and..."

"I get it!" He growled. "You're not hungry so the rest of us have to starve. Fucking typical! You're nothing but a selfish bitch."

"Gary keep your voice down you're going to wake Jason."

"Why would you care if he wakes up? You don't care about him…you'd prefer to sit on the fucking sofa and watch television rather than cook your husband a meal."

Tanya knew the only way out of having a massive explosion on her hands, was to drive the seven miles to the nearest all-night grocery store and pick up the two items he wanted. "Fine!" she growled as she headed for the front door. "But you'd better be up when I get back." After grabbing her keys from the table she flung open the door and stormed out.

By the time Tanya drove into the driveway it was one fifteen. Grabbing the bag, she quickly ran into the house and tossed her keys on the table. Gary was right where she thought he'd be, sleeping on the sofa with his mouth open and drool running down the side of his face. She debated for a few moments whether to cook his food, or just go to bed. Finally after tossing the two scenarios around in her head, Tanya decided to cook.

Once the food was ready and on the table, Tanya quickly cleaned the mess and woke Gary so he could eat. He stumbled sleepily into the kitchen, sat down and began eating his food. Tanya walked up the stairs and got ready for bed.

It was after two when Gary finally climbed the stairs and crawled into bed. He nudged Tanya to wake her. "Tanya, Tanya...wake up." He said loud enough to disturb the dead.

"What do you want now?" She asked in a sleepy tone.

"You have to get up and do the dishes. You know I don't like leaving the dishes in the sink overnight."

Her eyes popped open. "Why couldn't you wash your plate and silverware? I did all the other dishes."

"I can't believe you expect me to do your job" He growled. "I suggest you go downstairs and do the dishes."

Tanya tossed off the covers and climbed out of bed. She mumbled so low Gary couldn't hear her. "I swear you're the laziest man in the world."

He rolled over and fell asleep while Tanya cleaned the mess he left for her.

Chapter 36

Gary was sleeping when Tanya climbed out of bed to get Jason ready for school. She barely had the energy to make his breakfast and get them both dressed and out the door. By the time she returned to the house she was ready to take a quick nap. She spied the slip of paper with Thomas' phone number, and couldn't believe how careless she was to leave it in plain sight. After sliding the small note into her pocket, Tanya climbed out of the car and entered the house

Gary was sitting at the table reading the newspaper when she walked in. When she entered the kitchen, Tanya released a heavy sigh knowing there would be no time for her to go back to bed. "What are you doing up?" She asked as she grabbed a coffee mug from the cabinet. "I thought you didn't have school until later today."

Gary glanced up from his reading. "I'm sorry; I didn't realize I needed your permission to get out of bed." He said with his usual sarcastic tone.

"I didn't mean anything; I had just assumed you'd stay in bed later since you were up so late last night."

He returned to reading the paper but not before he growled out an order. "I need another cup of coffee." He held his mug up for her to take.

After pouring his coffee she took her own cup into the living room to relax while she watched the news. Gary entered the room a few moments later with his cup in hand. "Where's the remote?"

Tanya frowned and handed him the small device. Knowing he would flip through the channels, Tanya rose to her feet and walked out of the room. She always hated it when he scanned through the stations. He would stop long enough on one channel to get her interested in a program, and then he would change it again. She walked into the kitchen, sat down on a chair and rested her arms and head on the table. Being exhausted and knowing she had to work until midnight, she thought she could get a few minutes of rest before Gary demanded her to do something else.

An hour past when Gary entered the room and noticed Tanya had fallen asleep. He growled. "What the hell! How could you be sleeping? I swear you're the laziest fucking bitch."

Tanya lifted her head. She had had enough of Gary's inconsideration. She was in no mood to listen to his rude comments. She stood up, placed her mug in the sink and turned to face him. "Well let me just get one thing straight right now. If I didn't have to wait on you hand and foot, I'd probably have gotten a fair amount of sleep last night. But because you decided you needed me to go to the store and cook your meal…" She tossed her hands in the air. "If you ask me you're the most inconsiderate asshole…"

He stopped her ranting. "Oh now here it is, you're complaining about having to do a few things after work. Well, let me be the first to inform you, I do my fair share around here. Who do you think does the laundry?"

Tanya glared at him. She knew she wouldn't have taken on an argument so early in the morning, but she was at her wits end. Not having enough sleep always caused her to be a bit testy. "You fucking wash and dry the clothes. You leave them on the sofa in a ball for me to fold and put away when I get out of work. I have even seen you parking your ass on the heap because you refuse to sit on the chair. If you ask me…you're far more worthless than I am!" She knew by the look on his face he was going to throw a fit.

Gary took two long strides, grabbed the newspaper he had left on the table and shredded it, tossing the bits of newsprint on the floor in the process. Tanya watched as his anger turned into rage and she began to tremble. He turned toward her and bellowed, "You fucking worthless piece of shit! How dare you say I do nothing around here! I work my ass off taking care of your kid while you go to work and do what…relax behind a desk and do nothing."

"That's right Gary, they pay me to just sit there and do nothing all night! You're such a fucking jerk!"

He scanned the length of her body and spied the small scrap of paper with Thomas' phone number on it. He grabbed her pocket, pulled out the paper and stared down at the seven digits. "What's this?" he growled. "Is this some worthless piece of shit you call a friend?"

Tanya shrugged. "I have no idea whose number that is."

"Well idiot with a pea for a fucking brain, maybe I should call it to see who answers."

Tanya didn't say a word. She just remained where she was and didn't allow his threat to faze her. If the truth had been known, she wished he called. At least then he would've been concerned knowing another man was interested in his wife. Instead he turned on the gas stove and held the paper close to the blue flame. While the small scrap of paper burned he laughed. "Guess you and your friend won't be chatting on the phone today." He tossed the burning remains in the sink and walked out of the room.

Two weeks had passed since Thomas gave Tanya his phone number. Every hour he would make his rounds, and every hour he'd stop at Tanya's department to talk to her for a few minutes. Tanya was getting tired of her work day being interrupted by him, but she never said a word. She was afraid he'd lash out in the same manner Gary always did.

Tanya stood in the hallway staring out the window. She was always relaxed during work. There was no one to ridicule her every move, no yelling and screaming going on. Work was always a peaceful retreat for her. She momentarily closed her eyes and enjoyed the quiet solitude.

Her eyes popped open the moment she heard footsteps echoing down the adjacent hallway. Her stomach clenched when the heavy footsteps neared the corner. Tanya knew Thomas was doing his rounds and lately he was always talking to her about sex which made her uncomfortable. Turning to glance at the department clock, she realized the five minutes of alone time had been spent at the wrong time.

Thomas rounded the corner just as Tanya was reaching for the door. "Hey beautiful." He smiled brightly when Tanya turned to look at him.

Scowling, she twisted the knob and shoved the door open. Thomas was standing beside her with his foot in the doorway making it impossible to shut. "Tom, I have to get back to work."

"Oh I think you can spare a few minutes to spend with me."

She stared down at the floor. "Look, I'm not in the mood to talk."

He reached up and placed a hand on her breast. "Maybe you're in the mood for a little playtime."

Tanya shoved his hand away and growled. "What the hell do you think you're doing?"

"Come on Tanya, you and I both know your husband isn't taking care of you...let me do the job he can't. I can please you the way a man should please his woman."

Tanya's stomach clenched so hard it caused sharp pains to radiate from the center of her abdomen up through her chest. The metallic taste of blood erupted from her throat. She held an arm protectively across her stomach and waited for the pain to subside. "Tom, please leave me alone. I don't want to have sex with you. I'd appreciate it if you'd let me close the door so I can get back to work."

Thomas knew by the look on Tanya's face something was wrong. Her face drained of all color and he knew she was in pain. "Tanya, are you alright?" a hint of panic was in his voice."

"I'm fine. Just go away." He stepped away from the door and allowed her to close it.

While walking to her desk, Tanya's stomach threatened to spew its contents. She knew she couldn't hold it in much longer so; she bolted for the ladies room. She made it just in time to spew bright red blood and black granules into the toilet. She wiped her mouth with a wad of toilet paper. The pain in her stomach increased. She would've loved to go home, but since Gary was there, she decided against it.

By the time it came to the end of her shift, Tanya was ready to go home and go to bed. She felt weak ever since the vomiting incident. Her stomach growled, but she didn't think she should eat until the pain subsided.

As she walked out of the building she noticed Thomas standing beside her car. *Damn it! What the hell does he want?* She thought as she approached her car. She scowled at him. "Tom, I'm not in the mood to hear any shit. I'm not going out with you and I'm not having sex with you. So unless you have something intelligent to discuss, please leave me alone."

Thomas looked confused. "I'm not going to ask you out, I just want to know how you're feeling. I heard you spent a while in the ladies room and…"

"Who would tell you that? I'll bet Clara told you. She has such a big mouth sometimes," She glared at the ground.

[225]

"I promised I wouldn't say. Tanya I just want to know if you're all right."

She pushed passed him and to unlock her door. "I'm fine. I just need to go home and relax." *If that's possible.* She thought as she slid the key into the lock. The sharp pains in her stomach started to blossom again. She opened the door and climbed in.

Thomas held the door, leaned in and said "I'm sorry if I had anything to do with your illness."

"Tom just let it go." She placed her hand on the door pull and tugged. Thomas continued to keep his hold on the door.

"When can I see you…ah I mean outside of work."

Exasperated Tanya stared up into his pleading eyes. "I'm married, and just because Gary's not the greatest guy in town, it doesn't mean I'd cheat on him. Please just leave me alone."

Thomas released his hold on the door while saying, "I'm not giving up. I'll keep hounding you until you say yes,"

Tanya closed the door, started the car and drove away.

By the time she arrived home her stomach pains had started to subside. The usual tension she felt during the twenty minute ride sat on the back burner and threatened to escalate at any given moment. Tears rolled down her cheeks when she remembered the amount of blood her stomach spewed. *What would cause a person to vomit blood?* She thought as she parked the car in the driveway.

When she entered the house, it was unusually quiet. She released a sigh and wondered if it was the lull before the storm. As she entered the kitchen she noticed a bouquet of flowers. A note was propped against the crystal vase. She lifted the sheet of paper and read:

Tanya,
I want to tell you how sorry I am for the way I treated you yesterday.
Please forgive me, I love you
Gary

Tanya was shocked when she read his apology. Although she knew it wouldn't last as long as the flowers would, she needed something to ease her stress and the flowers seemed to do the trick.

She didn't hear him walk into the room. He cleared his throat and said, "Babe, I heard you were sick at work today."

Dumbfounded she wondered who would've told him. Sure she spent almost an hour in the ladies room, but she didn't think anyone, who knew she was sick, would call Gary. She turned to face him. "Who told you?"

Clara, the girl you work with called and said I'd better take it easy on you because you were in the bathroom throwing up. Is it true…you vomited at work?"

Tanya stared down at the floor. The all too familiar pains began to blossom in the pit of her stomach. "Yes it's true." She said as if she were ashamed.

Gary approached her, "Why didn't you come home?"

She didn't want to tell him it was because he was here. "I had a lot of work to do. I needed to get a few things off the line and ready for shipment." She looked into his eyes. "Gary, I'm being sexually harassed at work. I think I should take my complaint to the personnel department."

Gary looked like he wanted to laugh. She knew he wanted to say something nasty but for once he held tongue. "You can't cause waves at work. You'll get fired and then what are we supposed to do?"

"I can't let this guy keep saying the things he says. He's constantly asking me out even though he knows I'm married."

Gary held back his laughter as long as he could. "Let me give you a little tip. This little fantasy of yours isn't working. For your information there isn't a man on this planet that would put up with you and your bullshit. Face it Tanya, there isn't anyone asking you out." He turned and walked out of the room.

Tanya slumped down in a chair and stared at the bouquet that seemed to be mocking her. Tears welled in her eyes and she finally realized Gary was right she was worthless. She imagined Gary convinced Thomas to approach her with kind words just to see what she would say. She rose to her feet, dried her eyes and went to bed.

Chapter 37

By the time Tanya had been married for eleven years, things had changed drastically. She no longer worked nights. Gary had a decent job working second shift, but his attitude toward Tanya never wavered. Where it stood, Tanya only talked to Gary if he asked her a direct question. She never added to a conversation and never voiced her opinion out of fear he'd call her some demeaning name. She had learned from past experiences the aggravation just wasn't worth it.

Gary came home one night in his usual, nasty, rude and spiteful mood. It was like the man was never happy. He played his usual 'I'm going to wake up Tanya and treat her like shit' role and as usual Tanya was forced to put up with it.

Tanya heard him the moment he stepped into the dark room. She pretended to sleep, silently hoping he would leave her alone. He bellowed his usual commands. "Tanya, get the hell out of bed and cook my dinner."

Tanya moaned, "Gary, I made dinner…I always make you dinner."

"You made the type of shit I wouldn't feed a fucking dog."

She proper herself up on an elbow. "Funny you didn't say that three weeks ago when I made the same thing. As a matter of fact you said you loved pasta fagioli....you got the recipe from your grandmother...or don't you remember doing that."

"I don't remember telling you I wanted to eat that every fucking day."

She flopped back down on her pillow and let out a huge sigh. "Fine, what do you want?"

Gary leaned against the door jamb, crossed his arms over his chest and thought for a brief moment. He was always so dramatic when he would tell her what he wanted. "Why don't you come down and make us some fried chicken."

"Chicken? You want me to make fried chicken in the middle of the night?"

"What the hell Tanya! You asked me what I wanted and when I tell you, you blow a fit."

She tossed the covers off and climbed out of bed. "I didn't think you'd want something that would take an hour to cook. I was going to make that for tomorrow's dinner."

"Well make it tonight, and then you and Jason can have the leftovers tomorrow."

Knowing there was no end to his battling; Tanya walked downstairs and prepared the meal he requested. Once she was done, she cleaned the dishes and went back to bed.

On Friday afternoon Gary said, "Marcus and Lily are coming for dinner tomorrow. I thought we'd have a duck with the orange sauce...what do you think?"

Tanya shrugged. "What time are they coming?"

I told them to be here around six-thirty. That should give you enough time to get everything prepared."

"That's fine." was all she said. She pulled out a cook book and found a great recipe for duck. After making the shopping list, she gathered her coupons and headed for the front door.

Gary halted her just before the door closed. "Where are you going?"

Pausing at the door, not willing to turn to face him, she said, "I'm going to get the stuff for your dinner tomorrow."

Gary had a hint of irritation in his tone. "Now? It's almost dinner."

Tanya turned to face the irritating man. "You told me not thirty minutes ago you invited your friends for dinner tomorrow. Unless you want to have chicken, I have to go to the store to purchase the stuff I'll need to make your dinner."

"I don't know why you're bitching. I was just asking...go ahead and go, just make sure you get back here in time to cook tonight's dinner."

Tanya knew she was snippy, but she was tired of his attitude. Eleven years of being treated like a servant was weighing heavy on her. She couldn't figure out what mood he would be in from one minute to another. She stepped out the door and went on her merry way. Any time without Gary was a good time as far as Tanya was concerned.

Gary was sitting on the sofa watching television, as usual, when she walked in the door with four plastic grocery bags hanging from her hands. The rustling of plastic and the banging of canned goods against the door caused Gary to pry himself away from his program and rush to the foyer. Instead of helping her with her heavy burden, he scowled. "What the hell is all this?" He asked while pointing at the parcels.

"It's the stuff for your dinner tomorrow."

Gary pulled one of the bags from her hand and dumped it on the floor. He leaned down and picked up a jar. "What the hell do we need fucking peanut butter for? The last time I ate peanut butter I was fucking ten."

Tanya grabbed the jar from Gary's hand, carried it and the remaining bags in her hands to the kitchen. "For your information Jason asked me to pick this up. I know you think you're the only one who lives in this house, but in reality, you're not."

"What the fuck are you talking about? I know I'm not the only one here, but if the truth would be told, I wish I was."

Tanya tossed the bags on the table and stormed out of the room. Quickly she ran up the stairs and slammed her bedroom door. Gary flew up the stairs behind her and was immediately halted when he tried to open the locked door. He heard her slamming items around and her muffled growls. All of a sudden she tore open the door, pushed passed him and raced to the bathroom. Blood and black granules landed on the floor beside the toilet.

Tanya heard Gary in the hallway with his fake sympathy claiming he was sorry as she cleaned the mess, tears flowed down her face. She knew throwing up blood, although normal for her, wasn't a normal occurrence the average person suffered. Lately every time Gary upset her she would spend time in the bathroom either cleaning the blood off the floor or flushing the bloody mess down the toilet.

She wished she could go to him and explain what was going on, but she knew in the long run, he wouldn't care. Tanya felt her life and health always had to take a backseat. The blood on the floor didn't change her mind about her medical situation. Instead of calling the doctor or going to the emergency room, Tanya took antacids and prayed the pain would go away.

Gary stood outside the bathroom with his forehead pressed against the door. Jason, who was with Gary's mother, entered the house. He was excited about some toy his grandmother bought him and in his excitement he ran through the house in search of Tanya. "Mom, are you home?"

Tanya heard her son's excitement and she wanted to go see what was going on, but she didn't have the strength to raise herself off the bathroom floor. She heard Gary say, "Jason, go downstairs. Mommy's in the bathroom she'll be right down."

Jason knew there was something wrong. "Why are you standing there staring at the door? Is mommy alright?"

Gary was getting upset with his son's questioning. "She's fine! Just go downstairs and wait...she'll be down in a minute."

Tanya heard Jason stomping down the stairs. Finally after a few long moments she rose to her feet, flushed what little blood made it into the toilet, cleaned the towel she used to wipe up the mess and left the bathroom. He watched her as she brushed past him.

Gary and Tanya didn't speak for the rest of the evening. The clothes she was going to pack were left in the small suitcase. Gary knew he had pushed her too far, and he also knew something happened to her in the bathroom. Not really caring to investigate, he walked down the stairs and made Jason's dinner.

Tanya was asleep when Gary climbed on the bed and placed his hand gently on her shoulder. He whispered, "Babe, are you awake?" Tanya moaned. "Tanya, can you wake up and talk to me for a minute?"

Tanya's eyes opened, her back was to him. She stared at the wall. "What do you want?"

"I was in the bathroom and I noticed splatters of blood on the wall...did you cut yourself?"

"No Gary, I didn't cut myself." She clenched the covers in a ball and held them close to her chin. "Just leave me alone, I'm fine."

She felt his weight leave the bed and a wave of relief washed through her tense body. "I'll be downstairs if you need anything." He said softly as he walked out of the room. "I love you." He stepped through the door shutting it behind him.

The next day Jason had plans to sleep at a friend's house. He was excited because he was finally allowed to take a few of his favorite video games with him. As he packed his bag to leave, he stared into Tanya's eyes. "Mom, do you feel alright? You look kind of sick."

Not knowing what to say and not wanting to make him worry she said, "I think I have a little stomach bug. I'll be fine in a couple of hours. I want you to mind your manners and listen to Mr. and Mrs. Dillon. When they tell you to go to bed, I want you to go without a fuss. I know how kids your age are when they have a little time away from their house."

"Mom, you worry about everything I promise I'll be good. Mr. Dillon's going to take us out for pizza. He gave me and Mike a choice of anything we wanted to eat…and we decided we wanted pizza. He's a really nice dad…" Jason's voice softened. "Not like my dad."

Tanya's heart ached for her son. She knew he wanted to spend time with Gary, but Gary always had an excuse. "Well your father's very busy. I'm sure if you ask him, next week he'll take you fishing."

"Yeah, he always says he'll take me, but he never does." Jason was picking at the plastic encasing the duck. "I just wish he was more like other dads."

Tanya looked into her son's eyes. "I can talk to him if you really want him to take you someplace."

Jason shook his head. "You don't have to. I know how he gets when you try to make him do stuff with me. I don't want him to yell at you because of me."

[237]

She leaned down and gave him a kiss on the top of his head. "Maybe we can go fishing. I used to fish all the time when I was a kid." She crinkled her nose. "You'll have to deal with the worms though…I can't bring myself to touch them."

Jason chuckled. Gary walked into the room and stared down at the duck. "I can't wait to have dinner tonight." He placed his hand on Jason's shoulder. "Do you have everything? I'm not going to bring anything you forget, so you'd better make sure you take everything you'll need."

Jason looked at Tanya before he said, "I have everything. If you want me to stay home mom…ah I will."

Tanya smiled. "No I want you to go and have a good time. I'll see you tomorrow. If you need anything you can call me…" She glanced at Gary out of the corner of her eyes. "I don't want you to ever feel like you can't call me…or your father."

Gary smiled. "Okay Jason, let's get going. I know you must have a busy evening planned."

A half hour before Gary's guests were to arrive, the phone rang. Gary was sitting in his usual spot on the sofa. He said, "I'll get it." As he placed his hand on the receiver he said, "I hope that's not Jason."

Tanya was basting the duck when he entered the room. "Mark and Lily aren't coming. That was Marcus, he said Lily has a stomach bug and she didn't want to give it to us." He slammed his fist down onto the counter. "He could've come alone. Who the hell wants that whiny bitch around anyway?"

Tanya nearly burned herself on the pan when he pounded his fist onto the counter. "Gary, some men like to help their wives when they're sick. You know not all men think women are worthless."

Gary scowled. "How long before that piece of shit is ready?"

"It's done; I'm just letting it rest while I mash the potatoes."

Gary grabbed a plate and utensils and placed them on the table. He growled. "Why the fuck did you cook all this food?"

She pushed the beaters into the mixer. "If you remember correctly, we were supposed to have dinner guests. It was less than five minutes ago…"

Gary stepped toward her and Tanya backed away. She knew by the look in his eyes he was ready to throw a fit. She pressed her back against the counter and he stepped mere inches from her. His face was red with anger. Tanya's hands trembled. "I don't need you to tell me something I already know. I'm not the one with a brain of a mouse…you are.!" He stepped back and Tanya took that opportunity to walk out of the room.

The pain in her stomach blossomed as her tension increased. She knew she had to calm down or there would be another mess to clean in the bathroom. She sat on the sofa, hugged a pillow tight and waited for Gary's emotions to calm. She could hear the banging of pots and pans and the painful yell when she imagined he had burned himself, the image made her grin.

The kitchen was quiet so Tanya figured it was fairly safe to go into the kitchen and have a plate of food. She stood in the doorway stunned. Gary had eaten the entire duck, and tossed the potatoes and vegetables into the sink. Disappointment showed on her face. Gary glanced up from his plate and knitted his brows. "What the hell's wrong with you?"

"Oh nothing, I just thought maybe I could have dinner too, but I can see that's impossible, now that you ate the entire duck and you tossed the other shit into the sink. Did you even think for one minute maybe I'd like to have dinner?"

He scoffed. "By the looks of you, you can go a few weeks without eating. Believe me I did you a favor. Now you can have some of the salad you made." He rose to his feet, washed his face and hands in the sink with the vegetables and walked out of the room. Tanya was left to clean the mess he made.

Chapter 38

The Wednesday after the duck fiasco Tanya was putting laundry away when she found a few pieces of mail hidden in the bottom of Gary's sock drawer. She pulled them out and stared down at the address. The card had been addressed to her husband and delivered to a post office box. Tanya opened the flap and slid one of the cards out. Her heart skipped a beat when she read the card filled with phrases of love. After flipping the card open she read a hand written message also containing words of love elegantly scrolled.

Tears welled in her eyes, not for the fact a woman was in love with Gary, the tears were from the knowledge of her husband not valuing the sanctity of marriage. Tanya had always believed there was never a reason to have an affair. If one partner wasn't happy with the other, they should leave.

Tanya was the unhappy person in their marriage, and she suffered through everything Gary doled out. She stayed with him out of fear and the desire to have Jason live in a home with both parents. She dried her eyes, slid the card back into the envelope and left the room. Her heart ached, she had a decision to make and she had to make it before Gary returned from work.

While weighing her option the phone rang. Tanya lifted the receiver from the cradle and pressed it to her ear. "Hello?"

The strange voice on the other end of the line said, "Is this Mrs. Antonio?"

"Yes. May I ask who's calling?" Tanya said to the strange man on the phone.

My name is Robert Medina. I'm calling to inform you, your husband is having an affair with my wife. I know this must come as a shock to you, but I assure you I have proof and my wife confessed."

Tanya was at a loss for words. She sat down on the stairs just before her knees buckle. "Is your wife's name, Jessica?"

"Yes." The man's voice sounded confused. "You know about this?"

"I just found some cards a woman named Jessica had sent to my husband."

"From what I could get out of Jess, they've been having an affair for a little more than six months. I gave her an ultimatum; she's giving up your husband and staying with me. I want you to know, we'll be leaving the country...we're returning to Columbia so you have no worries about my wife stealing your husband."

Tanya was at a loss for words. She sat numbly on the stairs as she tried to regain her composure. "You're moving because your wife had an affair with my husband?"

The man chuckled. "No, but the move came at a good time. You see my mother has been very sick and I have to return to help take care of her. I've always been very close to her and I hate the idea of her being taken care of by anyone other than family. My sister has been carrying the burden for more than a year."

Tanya dried her eyes. "So your wife decided to stay with you? You can forgive her for the affair?"

"She's staying...I don't know if I'll ever forgive her, but marriage is sacred and we'll do whatever we have to stay together. Besides, she's not a citizen of this country. Jessica's here on a work visa and it expires soon. She has no choice; she has to go back with or without me." He paused for a brief moment. "I just want to tell you I'm sorry. I hope you can forgive my family for the wrong they have done."

Knowing the call was about to end, Tanya stood and braced herself on the banister. "I never met you, but I'm glad we had this conversation. Now I guess I have to deal with things on my end. Have a safe trip Robert and I wish the best for your mother."

"Thank you Mrs. Antonio. I'm glad there's no hatred between us." Robert Medina left her life as quickly as he had entered.

After pondering the situation for a few long moments, she came to a conclusion. Tanya called in sick and proceeded to make her hateful husband dinner. She cooked a meal Gary absolutely despised, called her mother in-law to pick up Jason and proceeded with her plan.

When she walked into the liquor store she wove through the isles in search of her husband's favorite wine. After making her purchase, Tanya returned home and continued with her preparations.

The table was set for one. A small bouquet of flowers had been placed in the center along with a pair of candlesticks. She turned off the light and the large kitchen was illuminated by the flame of the two candles. The cards Tanya found in his drawer were fanned out and lying on the cloth covered table in front of the bouquet.

It was a little after one a.m. when Gary finally stepped through the door. Thinking Tanya was being romantic he smiled. "What's all this?" He asked grinning ear to ear.

Tanya stood in the center of the doorway blocking Gary's view of the table. "Oh I thought I'd stay up to serve you dinner. You know I was thinking, you deserve to have a fresh hot meal when you get home from work."

The unsuspecting man pulled her into his arms and leaned his head down to kiss her soft lips. Tanya was repulsed by his display. She eased herself from his embrace. 'Why don't you take a seat while I prepare your plate?" She stepped aside to allow him entrance into the kitchen.

Gary spied the bottle of wine and immediately his smile turned into a frown. "What's going on Tanya? Why the wine and the candles?"

She hid her smile as he approached the table. "I just want you to know how special you are. Please have a seat."

Tanya knew the moment he recognized the cards. She smiled brightly. "What's the matter Gary? Why aren't you sitting?"

His face lost all its color. Tiny beads of sweat oozed from the pores on his forehead. He turned to face her. "You were in my drawer? How dare you go through my personal shit?"

"I didn't go through your stuff! I was putting laundry away."

Gary picked up the cards and flung them at her. "I don't know why you have to always make a mountain out of a mole hill. If I were you I'd spend a little more time taking care of the things you should be taking care of, and a lot less time on suspecting your husband of cheating on you."

"For your information…" Tanya's voice was calm when she explained. "A Robert Medina called me today. He said you and his wife have been carrying on an affair for the past six months."

Gary scoffed. "He's another one that doesn't know what he's talking about."

"Seems his wife Jessica…that is her name right? Anyway, it seems Jessica confessed to the affair and he called me out of courtesy. I guess there are some nice guys left in the world."

Gary glared at her, sat in his chair and spat out an order. "Just serve the fucking food. I'm tired of your fucking bullshit. I'd appreciate it if you'd shut your mouth long enough for me to enjoy my dinner…do you think you can do that, or is your minute pea brain overworking?"

Tanya smiled when she stepped to the stove with his empty plate in her hand. She neatly placed a mound of potatoes, a serving of peas and Gary's least favorite food in the world, meatloaf, on the pate. She turned and with a huge smile on her face she said "Enjoy." She placed the plate in front of him and walked out of the room.

She heard Gary's animalistic growl and the loud shattering of glass as the plate made contact with the wall. Smiling, Tanya walked into the living room, grabbed the luggage she had previously packed, and proceeded to walk out the door. *I hope he has fun cleaning the mess.* She thought as she gently closed the door behind her.

Realization slammed into Tanya's head as soon as she stepped onto the long narrow driveway. Although four cars could easily park nose to rear, there was no way to drive out of the driveway if someone happened to park behind you. Unfortunately for Tanya, Gary's truck was the last in line. The houses in the old neighborhood were close together. Shrubs lined one side and the house was on the other. There was no escape.

After deciding she would wait in her car until Gary went to sleep, move his truck and thereby allowing herself to vacate the driveway. Tanya stowed her suitcase in the trunk, turned and took her first step toward the driver's side when Gary flew out of the house.

Tears were flowing down his face. He grasped both of her arms and pleaded his case. "Please Tanya. You can't leave me. I know I'm not the best husband in the world and I know I've made mistakes…you have to understand I'm nothing without you."

Tanya scoffed. "Let me give you a little tip. You are far from the best anything. You have treated me like shit for eleven years and frankly I'm tired of it."

"I promise to change. I promise I'll treat you the way a husband is supposed to treat his wife. I love you Tanya. You can't leave…Please…I'm begging you." He ran his hands down the length of her arms. He stared deeply into her eyes, while he held her hands in his. "Come inside. I think we need to talk."

She tried to pull her hands from his tight grip. "I don't want to hear anything you have to say. I know you're just going to say things you think I want to hear. I'm tired Gary. I've put up with far more than any other woman…and I refuse to do it any longer."

"Babe, please give me a chance. Come inside and let me show you how much I love you." Gary stepped back and gave Tanya's hands a gentle tug. "I love you more than anything…if you leave me, I'll have no reason to live."

Tanya hated the way he manipulated her. She also hated the way she couldn't stand up to him. He terrified her and all she could think about was him turning his psychological abuse into something physical. She sucked in a deep breath, her hands began to tremble and the all too familiar pains in her abdomen erupted. She stared him down. "If I go in there, you have to promise me you're just going to talk."

"Yes, yes, I promise…we'll just talk." He tugged on her hands again and she stepped forward.

As soon as they entered the house Gary lead her to the living room, and eased her into the overstuffed chair. The only light in the room came from the foyer. He knelt down in front of her and stated his case.

It took two days for Gary to convince Tanya he would change. Tired of listening to his pleading words, Tanya finally said, "Alright, I'll stay! I just want you to know if I ever find out you've cheated on me again, there will be no talking yourself out of it. I'm willing to give you another chance with the understanding if you continue to treat me the way you have in the past…Jason and I are gone."

"I understand."

Gary promised Tanya the world the day she finally gave in. He promised to respect her and to love her for the person she was. He also swore the affair with Jessica was nothing more than sexual. Although it hurt Tanya to hear those words, she forgave him knowing she was worthless to any other man. Gary led her up stairs and the make-up sex was better than any intimate contact she had had in the past.

Chapter 39

Two months after the sexual encounter, Tanya was feeling tiny sensations in her abdomen. Every now and then she felt a strange pain. Not quite knowing what was going on, she made an appointment to see her gynecologist.

Tanya stood in front of the doctor's desk while he explained the situation "Mrs. Antonio, I'm happy to tell you…you're pregnant."

Her knees felt like rubber. She grasped the back of a chair just to keep herself standing. Her face turned white and the doctor's expression turned from bright and smiling to worry. He rose to his feet and rushed to help her into a chair. "Mrs. Antonio, you did know…I had you come into my office to give you the urine…correct me if I'm wrong…"

Tanya held up her hand to interrupt the doctor's stammering. "Dr. Flannigan, I…ah, don't quite know what to say. I didn't come here for a pregnancy test. Your nurse told me it was routine. I…" She covered her face with her trembling hands and murmured, "I want a second opinion."

Dr. Flannigan chuckled. "Tanya there's no need for a second opinion when it comes to pregnancy. You either are pregnant, or you're not. In your case, you are."

A tear welled in her eye. Jason was ten; he was old enough to be left alone for an hour or two. She wondered how she was going to start all over, raising an infant in a marriage that was rocky at best.

She rose to her feet, thanked the doctor and started to walk out of the room. "Mrs. Antonio, if you don't want to…"

She turned and gave the man a cold penetrating stare. "I know what you're going to say. I refuse to have an abortion. I'm a big girl and I can handle this. It's the initial shock that caused me to act the way I did."

"I'll need to see you in a month. Here's a prescription for pre-natal vitamins. If you have any questions or concerns don't hesitate to call."

Tanya took the prescription from his hand, walked out the door and made an appointment.

By the time Tanya arrived home, she pretty much accepted the fact she was pregnant. She wasn't quite sure how Gary would take the news, but she was happy. Once the initial shock wore off, she no longer felt overwhelmed. Stepping out of the car, she grabbed her purse, the prescription and made her way to the front door.

Gary was getting ready for work when she walked in. He glanced up from the ironing board, something he had agreed he would do from now on, and smiled. "How did your appointment go?"

She slid her purse off her shoulder and placed it on one of the kitchen chairs. "Well it was shocking to say the least."

Gary placed the iron on its heel and approached her. He pulled her into his arms and kissed her tenderly. "Tell me what the doctor said. Is everything alright?"

Tanya couldn't believe how different Gary had been ever since she found out about the affair he had had with Jessica. He was attentive and loving. He respected her and helped her around the house with various chores. In the two months since the incident he was a changed man. The only thing Tanya realized was, Gary could return to his old way of thinking at the drop of a hat. She just didn't know what would make him snap. She bit her lip. "Well, there's nothing wrong. I have to take this prescription." She handed him the small white bag containing the prenatal vitamins. "She said I'm...ah...pregnant."

Gary stepped back and eyed her suspiciously. "Pregnant? How could that be?"

She pulled out a chair and sat down. "Please don't look at me as if I've grown a second head. I was as shocked as you are."

Tanya knew Gary was about to snap. He looked down at the bag that held the pill bottle. "I honestly don't know what to say. Is he sure?"

"I asked the same question. I even asked to get a second opinion…there's no mistake Gary, I'm pregnant."

The pregnancy pill didn't go down easy for Gary. Tanya knew he was holding back his temper with all the strength he could muster. He placed the bag on the table and returned to his ironing without saying another word.

Two weeks had past and the topic of Tanya's pregnancy never made it into their conversations. She had assumed Gary thought if he ignored the situation it would go away. She followed the regime faithfully, taking the vitamins as directed and avoiding stress.

Gary came home from work one evening with an attitude. Tanya was asleep when he entered the room. "Get the fuck up!" He bellowed.

Not expecting his loud voice, Tanya bolted up straight in bed, turned her wide eyed gaze toward him and said with a yawn, "What the hell! Why did you have to wake me up like I'm some kind of animal?"

Gary stared into her sleepy eyes. "Get the hell up and make me something to eat."

"I left you a plate in the refrigerator. Didn't you see it?"

"I don't want that fucking garbage. Get up and make me some real food."

Stunned, Tanya climbed out of bed and walked downstairs with Gary close on her heels. She removed the plate from the refrigerator and held it out for him to see. "I don't know what you want. I made the fish you asked for. I even went out of my way to make scalloped potatoes…what the hell is wrong with this?"

He tossed his hands in the air. In doing so, he hit the plate and it flew out of Tanya's hand, landed on the floor and shattered. Tears welled in her eyes. "I can't believe you did that!" She crouched down and started picking up the pieces. "Why would you slap a dish out of somebody's hand? If you didn't want it, Jason would've eaten it. I swear you're like a spoiled three year old."

Gary stepped forward and placed his foot on a rather large portion of the broken plate. Under his weight, the fragment of the plate broke into smaller pieces and the potatoes were smeared onto the floor. She glanced up at the menacing man towering above her. "Shut your fucking mouth and clean up that pig slop." He stepped away from the mess, pulled open the freezer and removed a steak. He tossed it on the table causing Tanya to look up. "When you're done cleaning that mess, cook the steak…I'll be in the living room watching television while I wait."

I knew it...the nice attitude couldn't last forever.
She thought as she continued to clean the
mess. As soon as the new meal was cooked,
she entered the foyer, placed her right foot on
the first step and said as she started to climb
the stairs, "Your food is on the table. Now if
you don't mind I'm going back to bed."

Gary walked past the stairs on his way to
the kitchen. He mumbled a snide remark that
Tanya couldn't hear and frankly she didn't
care. She listened to the clatter of silverware
clinking on a plate and quickly fell back to
sleep.

The next few weeks were very rough.
Between morning sickness, Jason's lashing out
about the pregnancy and Gary acting like a
total ass, Tanya wondered if the child would
ever be accepted by anyone other than her.

By the six month mark of the pregnancy,
Gary was starting to come around. He was
actually looking forward to the birth of their
daughter. He thought of many outlandish
names, but finally settled on the name
Cassandra. As the child grew the doctor's
became more and more concerned about
Tanya's lack of weight gain. After testing her
for various illnesses, he discovered she had
gestational diabetes. Tanya was concerned,
but as long as the child remained healthy and
she ate right the doctor wasn't very
concerned.

When Tanya returned home from her latest appointment, Gary was at the door waiting. "What did the doctor say? Is Cassandra alright?"

She placed her purse on the small table beside the door along with her keys and her prescription refill. "The baby's fine. I have gestational diabetes, which is causing me to lose weight. He doesn't seem very concerned, so I guess I shouldn't be."

Gary smiled. "I guess I should've gotten you pregnant a long time ago. If we had a few more kids maybe you'd be a normal weight. In other words, losing weight for you is a good thing. I know, why don't you stop eating for a few months, or at least until the baby is born...you could actually come out of this looking good."

Tanya scowled at his rude remark. "Do you always have to be such an asshole?" Tears welled in her eyes but she refused to allow Gary to have the satisfaction in knowing he ripped away another layer of self-esteem from her. Gary's idea of the perfect woman, she had to be five foot ten and weigh as much as an average ten year old. In other words the woman had to be a walking skeleton.

"I'm merely stating a fact. If you can't take the truth..."

"You know what? I've had quite enough of your rude comments. From now on, I'd appreciate it if you only talked to me if you have something important to say. In other words asshole, I only want to hear things concerning Jason...nothing more." Tanya stormed out of the room. She noticed the look on Gary's face as she climbed the stairs.

As she lay weeping on the bed, Gary entered the room. "I'm sorry; I didn't mean to hurt your feelings. Please Tanya calm down...you know I love you. You being upset can't be good for the baby."

Those three little words were getting harder and harder for her to swallow. Tanya knew whenever Gary said "I love you" it was because he thought they would make her melt and her anger and the pain she felt would wash away. Her body cringed at the sound of his voice. Lately every time he touched her, her skin would crawl. She wept through his pitiful apology. The words he spoke meant nothing to her.

Twelve years of apologizing, only to have his sharp words slash at her heart and her irreparable psyche. She was a shell, nothing more. If it hadn't been for Jason, she would've ended her worthless miserable life years ago.

He rounded the bed and crouched down in front of her. "Tanya baby, please...I don't know why I said the things I did. I love you." He kissed her cheek and ran his fingers through her hair. "I swear I'll never say a mean thing to you again. I was stressed, I wasn't thinking. Honey, please I love you."

Tanya murmured. "Just go away. I don't want to hear your meaningless apology. You do this shit all the time and I'm sick of it."

He rose to his feet and sat on the bed beside her. "My apology isn't meaningless. What do I have to do to prove it?"

"You can start by leaving me alone."

He rose to his feet and walked out of the room without uttering another word.

Chapter 40

Gary was outside working in the yard when one of the neighbors approached him. He glanced up from his weeding to greet the man. "Hey Chris, how are things going?"

Tanya was busily watering the plants on the three season porch, when Chris made his appearance. She pause her watering task and eyed the peculiar man. His dark hair was disheveled and his brown eyes darted nervously from side to side. "Things are going good." He had a hint of tension in his tone. Tanya knew by the look on the man's face he was about to confront Gary about something…she continued to watch.

"How's your wife doing? I haven't seen her around."

"Look I didn't come here for small talk. I know this isn't my business, but I couldn't help noticing over the past few months you've been treating Tanya like shit."

Gary scowled. He always hated to be seen as anything other than the best person in the world with the kindest heart, so Chris' words cut him deep. "I'm not sure I know what you mean. I love my wife. She's the best thing that has ever happened to me."

"You might love her, but that doesn't change the fact you treat her like garbage. I can't tell you how many times I've passed this house and heard you belittling your wife. To tell you the truth there have been so many times I've wanted to bust down the door and beat the living shit out of you. Tanya's a great person with a big heart. I suggest you stop with your badgering. The next time I hear you yelling at her, I'm going to have to call the police." With that said Chris turned on his heels and walked away.

Gary stood in the middle of the flower garden with the look of consternation on his face. Tanya pulled her eyes away from him knowing if he spied her looking at him she would have hell to pay. He picked up his garden tools, shoved his soil caked gloves in his back pocket and walked to the backyard. Once he was out of sight Tanya released a huge sigh. She never knew Chris, or anyone else for that matter, heard Gary's name calling and taunting. She also didn't know if Gary would listen to the man's words or if he would turn his anger on her.

Tanya finished watering the plants and entered the house. Gary was sitting at the table with his head in his hands. He glanced up as soon as he heard her enter the room. His tone was soft, but his words were harsh. "If I find out you've been telling the neighbors that I treat you like shit…I'll fucking kill you."

"I don't know what you're talking about. I never talk to anyone. The only person I speak to is Mrs. Larson."

"Well someone said something to Chris. He came here and accused me of abusing you. I swear if I find out you've been crying to the neighbors…I'll…I'll divorce you."

Tanya raised an eyebrow. She didn't want him to see the threat he just spoke would be a blessing. Although she never spoke to anyone about the way Gary treated her, she thought it might be a great time to start. "I don't know why you're accusing me. You told me a long time ago not to speak to people outside your family. As a matter of fact I'm surprised I can talk to my mother. You hate her and…"

Tanya's voice raised a couple octaves when Gary rose to his feet and loomed over her in a threatening manner. His hands were clenched and his face was so red it had a purple hue. He growled through his teeth, "If I were you, I'd stop yelling at me. I may have never hit you in the past, but that doesn't mean I won't start." He left the kitchen and ran around the entire house closing every open window.

Gary cooled down a few days later and it appeared Chris' little talk changed him. It was as if something inside him snapped. He couldn't deny the fact he was mean to Tanya.

Chris made it perfectly clear he knew, so Gary wondered how many other people knew who didn't have the guts to approach him.

Chapter 41

Cassandra's delivery day was planned due to the constant contractions Tanya was suffering through. The doctor thought inducing labor would be safer for the baby. Two weeks early, Tanya and Gary sat in a birthing room waiting for the medication to take effect.

Gary sat in a chair and watched as the nurse prepped his wife for the inoculation. During the six hours of labor, Gary never once gave Tanya an encouraging word. He did however discuss recipes with the nurse. Gary scowled down at Tanya when the labor pains became intense. He said, "Tanya, stop being a baby. I know it can't hurt as bad as you're making it out to be."

The nurse's jaw dropped. She growled. "Are you kidding? Of course it hurts! Why don't you go home and try shitting a watermelon. When it's over, you can come back here and tell me how easy it was."

Gary clamped his mouth shut and sat down. Tanya knew he was embarrassed, but he really shouldn't have spoken concerning something he knew nothing about. The labor lasted another twenty minutes. As soon as the doctor made his appearance Gary stood at her bedside. Tanya knew he was trying to come across as the loving caring husband, but that little display didn't work for the nurse.

When their daughter arrived Gary was asked if he would like to cut the cord. Being the arrogant man he was, as he cut it he said, "I am the one who separated my daughter from my wife."

That statement made the nurse roll her eyes and the doctor stared into Tanya's eyes and just smiled.

Tanya's relationship with Gary although it had been horrible to this point, it started to spiral into the black abyss of no return. By the time Tanya's marriage reached the thirteenth year mark, Gary was spending more and more time out of state. Although his job required the occasional three week trips, she discovered he was volunteering to take the place of other coworkers.

Just before Cassandra's first birthday Gary approached Tanya with some information. They were in the kitchen drinking coffee and reading the newspaper. "I have to go out of state next week. There's a class everyone has to take and I decided if I was one of the first ones to go, it'll give me an edge on any promotions coming up in the future."

Tanya was always happy to hear when Gary was going away. She and Jason would spend time doing the things they loved and they could eat the things Gary always called 'slop'. To have Gary gone for a few weeks seemed like a vacation. She could relax and enjoy her life without the daily arguing. "Oh, when will you be leaving?" Tanya was smiling on the inside.

"Next Saturday. I figure I can get in and settled before the start of class on Monday."

That statement caused Tanya to wonder. "Why are you leaving so early?"

"Do I always have to have a reason? Why is it every time I have to go away you feel the need to question me? Stop your fucking bitching for once and be happy to know I have a decent job to keep your fucking ass in clothes. God knows you outgrow your clothes faster than the kids do." He laughed at his own rude comment.

You'd think after thirteen years of marriage Gary's bullying and hateful remarks would bounce off her, but if the truth had been told, he was pushing her further and further into a state of depression. "I wasn't questioning you, I was just wondering why. You usually leave on Sundays…believe me I'm not upset you're going."

Gary scoffed. "Why do you have plans to have your boyfriend over? Oh that's right; there is no man on this planet that would ever take you. If I were you, I'd consider myself lucky I have a nice guy like me."

Tanya rose to her feet, placed her cup in the sink and started cleaning the counter. She wanted to smack the smugness out of him, but she was terrified he'd retaliate. She thought as he ranted in the background, *I cannot wait until you're gone. I hope your fucking plane crashes. Hell with my luck, you'd be the only survivor. You'd stand up, brush yourself off and tell everyone your amazing story of survival.*

Tanya was shocked out of her private thoughts when Gary bellowed "Are you even fucking listening to me?"

"Sorry, I was just thinking."

"Well, don't fucking hurt yourself doing it. The kids are going to need the piece of shit they call mother. Boy am I glad I didn't have to deal with you growing up…you have to be the worst mother of the fucking planet."

Tanya tossed the dish rag onto the counter and glared at him. Tears welled in her eyes. He always seemed to know which nerve to pick on…and her being a poor mother was the one that hurt her the most. She glared at him as she walked past. "You know I think you should look at yourself once in a while. Maybe then you can see the man people see. I swear, you have to be one of the meanest assholes around." She stormed out of the room.

Gary rose to his feet and followed close behind. "I'm one of the nicest people you know. Hell I'm probably the only nice guy you know."

Tanya was on her way upstairs to attend to Cassandra when Gary spoke. Her foot was on the third step; she paused and stared down at him. "If you're the nicest man I know, I'd hate to meet the most spiteful. I swear you have this image in your head that you're God's gift to mankind."

Gary laughed. "I am. Although I can see you don't appreciate me."

She scoffed and ran upstairs to grab the baby.

It was Friday afternoon when Gary came to her place of work asking for her paycheck. "Tanya, you have to give me your check so I can cash it to have money for my trip."

Tanya being the idiot she was, handed it to him. "Don't forget to leave me money for the week since I won't have the checkbook." Gary always took the checkbook whenever he went away so he could pay the bills as soon as they came in.

He took her check and said, "Don't worry about it. You really don't think I'd leave you with nothing do you?"

Tanya shrugged and went back to work.

Saturday morning Tanya woke to the sound of Gary leaving. She looked at the clock and noticed it was seven fifteen. She rushed down the stairs and out the door. Gary was placing his luggage in the trunk. "Why are you leaving so early? I thought your flight wasn't until eleven thirty?"

"Oh…ah…I need to park in long term parking. It…takes a while to check in."

Tanya knitted her brows. "I thought I was taking you to the airport."

"Oh…ah…I thought it would be easier if I drove myself. This way the kids don't have to get up early and you can stay home and relax."

Gary was sliding into the car, paused and said, "I left money for you on the table. You're going to have to pick up diapers and a few groceries for the week. I love you. I'll see you in three weeks." He closed the door, started the engine and drove away.

Tanya stood on the porch with a dazed look on her face. *I know there's something going on. I hope he has a fucking girlfriend so I'll have a good excuse to leave him.*

Tanya turned and walked into the house. As she stepped into the kitchen she noticed the cash Gary had left on the table. She picked up the small pile and counted it. *Fifty dollars…how in the hell am I supposed to get everything we need with fifty dollars. He kept almost seven hundred for himself.* She was fuming. Tanya paced around the kitchen and growled out loud. "What the hell does he expect me to do with fifty bucks? I swear if that man had half a brain…" She growled. Tears welled in her eyes as she tossed the cash onto the table.

After brooding for a few long moments, Tanya decided two can play his game. She ran upstairs and pulled a check from the box of personal checks and decided she would go to the bank and withdraw cash for groceries. *He must've thought he left more. I'll just go get some money out of the account and tell him when he calls tonight.* Satisfied with her decision, she woke the kids and got them ready for a trip to the bank and the grocery store. She planned on surprising Jason with his favorite breakfast from McDonald's. After getting the kids in the car and driving to the bank, she said, "As soon as we leave here we'll go to get breakfast."

Jason smiled. "Can I play on the playground?"

Tanya smiled at her son in the rearview mirror. "Sure, then we have to go grocery shopping."

Jason made a face, but he was satisfied at least he would be able to spend a little time playing.

Tanya reached the drive-up window and slid the check under the bar to hold it in place. "Good morning." She said to the smiling teller. "How are you today?"

The teller smiled and began processing the check. A few moments later the woman said, "I'm sorry, but this account has been closed."

Tanya's jaw dropped. "What? You must be mistaken. We've had that account for years."

"It appears your husband closed this account a few days ago. Let me check...maybe he opened another joint account and forgot to tell you." Tanya rested her arm on the open widow. She was biting her nails while she watched the teller punch information into the computer. After a few long moments, the door slid open and the woman said, "I'm sorry, it seems Mr. Antonio opened an account in his name only." The woman had a sorrowful look on her face.

Tanya grabbed the worthless check and thanked the woman. As she drove out of the lot she peered into the mirror to look at her son. Not willing to disappoint her child and tell him he couldn't go to breakfast, she stared at his solemn face. "Change of plans Jason. Your father took all the money with him, so we just have to go to breakfast."

"Why did dad take all the money?"

"I don't know sweetie, but we'll be fine. We do have to stop for diapers before we go home."

Jason nodded and turned to glance out his window. "Dad's so mean sometimes."

"I know sweetie, but we'll do something special next weekend."

The entire three weeks Gary was gone, he called once to leave an emergency number on the answering machine. Tanya refused to call the number; she wanted to deal with him face to face, when he returned from his trip.

Chapter 42

When Gary returned home Tanya had devised a plan in her head. She wanted to confront him, before he was able to tell her the lies, he surely thought up during his time away. He had expected her to deposit money into their account, but that couldn't happen because the account was closed. Instead of keeping the cash in the house, Tanya opened her own account. Refusing to give Gary her entire paycheck, she decided she would only pay for groceries and he would have to ask her for money for a change.

When Gary entered the house, the only one who greeted him with a smile was Cassandra. He placed his carry-on on the floor, lifted his daughter into his arms and gave her a kiss. After a few brief moments he said in a cheerful tone, "Hello is my family here? Tanya, Jason I'm home."

Jason was in the living room playing a new video game. He refused to pull himself away long enough to greet his father. He knew the good mood would only last a few minutes so, in the world according to Jason, why bother."

Tanya was sitting at the kitchen table reading the newspaper. She pretended she didn't hear him come in. As he stepped into the room he said softly, "Babe, I'm home."

Tanya glanced up from her paper and gave him a half smile and went back to reading.

"What's wrong with you? I'd think after three weeks you'd at least be happy to see me." Gary had no idea Tanya knew about the bank account.

"Oh nothing's wrong; I'm just in the middle of reading this article."

Gary approached her and leaned down to give her a kiss. She leaned away from him and he scowled. "What the hell…I've been gone for three weeks and I can't get a decent welcome home?"

Tanya neatly folded the newspaper and pushed it aside. "Okay Gary, let me welcome you home. First, how was your trip?"

Gary smiled. "It was great. I finished top in my class and…"

"That's nice." She rose to her feet, stepped to the counter and turned to face him. She crossed her arms over her chest and scowled. "Maybe you can answer a few questions for me. First I'd like to know, how you expected me and the kids to get by with fifty dollars…not that we didn't, it was tight, but we survived." She paused for a few brief moments waiting for an answer, but all he did was glare at her. "Second, I'd like to know, why you closed the joint checking account.

Apparently you think you have total control over every dime that comes into this house."

Gary realized he was between a rock and a hard place. He listened to her questions, but she could almost see the wheels turning inside his head as he tried to think of reasonable answers. "Look, I meant to tell you about the checking account but it slipped my mind. You never write checks so I figured changing the account to get interest was the logical thing to do. Since you weren't around when I was at the bank, I did it…ah, spur of the moment. As far as leaving you only fifty dollars, I thought that would've been enough for you to get the minor things you needed. I didn't realize you needed more than milk and diapers."

Tanya listened to his pathetic explanations but refused to get caught up in his deceit. "Gary, you know, as well as I do, you had a motive for closing the account we had for years. As far as I'm concerned, you did it for control. You wanted to take my check weekly and deposit into your account and leave me with no access to the money I earned myself." His wheels were spinning again. She knew he didn't have a shovel big enough to dig him out of the hole he was in.

Gary began to laugh. "Tanya, you have no idea what you're talking about. Of course I wouldn't do that to you. I love you…you're my wife for Christ sake."

Tanya was fuming. "Just so you know we're both playing on the same field, I opened my own account."

"What? Why would you do that? Honestly Tanya, I never meant…"

"I know exactly what you intended on doing. Now you're upset because I caught you in your little devious plan."

Gary was getting more and more upset with each passing minute. His face turned red and tiny beads of sweat formed on his forehead. "I don't understand why you always have to look at things the way you do. I didn't think this would be a big deal to you. If it will make you happy, I'll open a joint account first thing Monday morning. Damn, you nitpick over everything." Gary walked out of the room to greet his son.

Tanya knew by the look on his face and the way he said 'I love you', there was another woman. *He has been using my money to entertain his girlfriend. He left me with nothing so he could show his 'friend' a good time. Well two can play that game.*

After putting the kids to bed, Tanya entered the living room and confronted him. "Gary, I need to know why you would put a woman above your family."

Gary glared at her. She knew by the look on his face and through past experiences of his infidelity that he was about to tell her a bold faced lie. He scoffed. "As usual you don't know what you're talking about." He turned back to watch the television.

"I know for a fact you have another woman. A man doesn't treat his family like shit unless he has something to hide. You seem to be forgetting, you've cheated on me in the past and I know all the warning signs."

He growled without looking in her direction. "Get out of my sight. Don't talk to me until you can apologize for all the shit you accused me of doing."

Tanya finally had the reason not to speak to him. She turned on her heels and walked upstairs.

The following week was peaceful. Gary did as he said he would, he kept his mouth shut. The tension in the air grew thicker with every passing day. Tanya was enjoying the idea of not being ridiculed every waking moment, but her stomach pains increased every time he was around her.

Friday was always a good day for Tanya. It was the day she got paid, and the day she would take Jason out for a little alone time together. They usually went out to dinner and then they'd catch a movie. He always loved the time he spent with his mother. Tanya soon realized their plans may come to an abrupt halt.

Gary showed up at Tanya's work just before it was the end of her shift. "I need to make a deposit." He held out his hand waiting for Tanya to give him her paycheck. "There are a few bills that have to be paid so I need your check."

She couldn't believe his gall. "I'm sorry; do we have a joint account now? The last I knew the checking account was only in your name."

"I told you I'd fix it and I will. I just haven't had time."

Tanya turned to walk away but not before she spied the smug smile on Gary's face. She paused, turned back to him and growled, "Until you get that little matter fixed, I won't b giving you my check. Tell me what bills need to be paid and I'll pay them."

"I don't know what they are. I just know bills will be coming in this week and they need to get paid."

She shrugged and leaned against the side of the building. "Well as soon as they come in, leave them on the table and when I get home Ill pay them. I refuse to give you my hard earned money, so you can take your girlfriend out on a date."

Gary sneered. "I don't have a fucking girlfriend. If I were you, I'd leave my check on the table so it can be deposited."

Tanya turned, opened the door and stepped inside leaving Gary standing in the parking lot with an angry expression on his face.

Chapter 43

The next few years were rough to say the least. Gary went on more and more 'business trips'. The only time he spoke to her was to ridicule or belittle her in some form or another. Her ego was broken and Tanya knew she would never be more than a shell. She only talked at work or whenever Gary wasn't around.

One day out of the blue Gary started talking. A mean or nasty comment never escaped his lips. He smiled when he told her all about the side job he was doing for one of his coworkers. She listened but never said a word. They had been married for seventeen years and in that time she knew whenever Gary mentioned a woman's name he was having an affair with her. He was like a teenager, constantly talking about his girlfriend. Gary didn't realize he did this, so when she heard the name Samantha roll off his lips, Tanya knew he was dating her.

"I have to go to Samantha's house to help her with a remodeling job. She asked me to hang sheetrock for her. Apparently her husband is worthless." Gary bragged as he continued. "Samantha always cooks me breakfast. So for the next few weeks don't expect to see much of me."

Tanya was surprised by the way he was acting and decided to add to the conversation. "I thought you hated Samantha. You always said she was an idiot."

He smiled. "Yeah well apparently I was wrong. She's' really very sweet, I don't know why she stays with her low life husband though…he's such a worthless man."

That was it, Tanya knew without a doubt he was cheating on her with yet another one of his coworkers. In the time he had been working at his job, there had been two affairs. All she had to do was to wait for him to slip up and leave behind the evidence. "Well maybe the guy just doesn't know how to do home repairs. Maybe he would rather hire someone to do them, rather than take the chance of doing it wrong."

"No, the guy doesn't do anything." Gary was sipping his coffee when he finally remembered something. After placing the cup on the table he said, "Oh yeah, I forgot to tell you, this weekend I'll be going out of town. I volunteered to take another class. I figure this will give me the edge on everyone. I always like to be one of the first people to take the classes…I'm more valuable that way. They won't fire me or lay me off if there's ever a layoff."

Tanya bit her lip. She knew Samantha worked the same shift and job as Gary. "Is...ah Samantha going?"

"Yeah they needed two of us to go, so we both volunteered." He could tell by the look on her face he said something that made Tanya suspicious. "We're not going together; we're just in the same class."

There it was the huge blunder she had been waiting for. "Does her husband know you two are going together?"

Gary rose to his feet and placed his cup in the sink. "I don't know. To tell you the truth, I don't think Samantha ever talks to him about the trips."

"Oh, they're not close?"

"I guess they are..." Gary was beginning to lose his temper. "Look I don't care about that asshole. As far as I'm concerned he can fall of the face of the earth."

He's jealous. She thought. Gary waited for her to say something, but she never did. He walked out of the room and started getting ready for work.

As soon as he left the house, Tanya began her investigation. She rummaged through all his usual hiding places for evidence of his affair and came up empty. Finally she started looking in his closet and lo and behold, there was a manila envelope filled with cards, receipts and various other memorabilia. The Cards were of the romantic variety, the receipts were for gifts of jewelry, dinners, and flowers. A tear welled in Tanya's eyes. She hadn't received flowers from her husband in years, and only then was it in the form of an apology for an affair.

She carried the large envelope to her dresser and slid it under a pile of blouses. She wiped her eyes and began to think.

She had had enough; she was going to confront him and let him know the marriage was over. Tanya could care less about Gary. He had been mean and spiteful their entire marriage and the arguing was taking its toll on her children. She devised her plan of attack. Not willing to give him the knowledge she had found his hidden things, Tanya came up with a way to make him squirm…he would have to ask her for the things to be returned.

Two days later Gary came to Tanya's place of work and called her outside. By the time she exited the rear door of the building he was in his car and he had a murderous look on his face. Tanya's stomach clenched as she approached the idling vehicle. She noticed Cassandra sitting in the back seat with a huge teardrop on her cheek. "What's going on?" She asked in a nervous tone.

"Why don't you tell me what's going on!" He growled through the open window. "I want my stuff back."

Tanya scowled, "What stuff?"

"The fucking stuff you took from my closet. I want you to give it back. You had no right…."

Tanya placed her hands on her hips. "No right! No right! Let me give you a little fucking tip! We're married; I have every right in the world to keep whatever I find in that house. If you didn't want me to find it, you should have hidden it outside of the house." She walked toward the front of the car to go give Cassandra a kiss. As soon as she rounded the passenger's side fender, Gary pressed his foot on the gas and rammed the car into her hip. The sudden jolt caused Tanya to lift off the ground, land on the hood and slide to the ground. As she was climbing to her feet she heard. "Give me back my fucking shit!" Gary sped out of the parking lot toward home.

A coworker, who was just arriving, rushed to Tanya's aid. "Tanya, are you all right? I saw that guy hit you."

Brushing dirt and debris from her clothes she said softly, "I'm fine. Gary's a little pissed at me, but I think he'll get over it."

"You should call the cops. He had no right to run you over."

Tanya limped painfully into the building. "I'm not calling the police. I'll work it out somehow. Besides he'll be leaving tomorrow on a business trip, so he'll have a couple of weeks to get over his anger."

You can't let him get away with that shit! I swear, if you don't call the cops...I will."

Tanya stared into the dark eyes of the younger man. His hair was a mess from scrubbing his hands over his head repeatedly. He paced the room. She calmly approached him. "David, I'll handle this. I'm working on a way to get out of the marriage. I don't want you to worry about Gary and what he might do."

David was totally frustrated with the entire incident, but he wanted to give Tanya the benefit of the doubt. He took three deep breaths before he spat out his next words. "I swear if he lays a fucking hand on you...I'll personally beat the living shit out of him!"

David was a muscular man who had a few good inches on Gary's five foot eleven height. Tanya nervously bit her lip. "I promise Dave, I'll be fine." She placed a hand on David's elbow. "Let's just go to work and forget about Gary."

Gary didn't return. All during the remainer of her shift, Tanya wondered what kind of hell her kids were going through. Remembering the tear on Cassandra's cheek, her eyes welled with tears. She hoped Gary would be out of the house before she returned home.

Chapter 44

By the time Tanya arrived home Gary was gone. He had left Cassandra in the care of her sixteen year old brother. When she entered the house Tanya called out their names. "Jason...Cassandra...mommy's home."

The two kids entered the foyer. Jason said, "Cass said dad hit you with the car."

Tanya placed her purse and keys on the small table. "I don't really want to talk about it right now." She let out a huge sigh. "How about, we go out for seafood tonight? I really feel like having someone wait on me for a change."

Jason smiled. He loved seafood and there was one particular restaurant in town he always wanted to visit. "Can we go to Cliff's?" His eyes were pleading.

"Sure, watch your sister while I take a quick shower and get ready. While I'm getting ready, I need you to get a set of sheets out of the linen closet and place them on the spare bed in Cassandra's room."

Jason scowled. "Why? Are we having company?"

"No sweetie, I'll be staying in there until your father goes on his trip."

By the time dinner was over and they arrived home, Tanya was beat. All she wanted to do was put Cassandra to bed and go to bed herself. She had dropped Jason off at a friend's house; he wasn't in the mood to hear his father yelling. Tanya yawned while she read a bedtime story. Once Cassandra was asleep, Tanya quickly made the bed, changed and climbed in. The tension of the day had dissipated during dinner.

Tanya was just about to fall asleep when Gary entered the house. Immediately she heard him growl. "If that fucking bitch knows what's good for her, my shit will be back in the closet. If not I'm waking her fucking ass up." He slammed the door.

Tanya heard him run up the stairs and scour his closet. She pulled the blankets over her head to muffle his ranting. A few minutes passed before she heard him try to open Cassandra's bedroom door. A deep growl escaped his throat when he realized the door was locked.

Gary ran down the stairs and started packing for his trip. She heard him talking on the phone. By the way he was talking; Tanya assumed the call was to Samantha. Curiosity got the best of her, so she climbed out of bed and stood at the head of the stairs. She heard, "…I told you before, I really don't think she'll take the shit to your husband. Besides she has no idea where you live." There was a few brief moments of silence before she heard, "We can talk about this in the morning when I pick you up." Silence, "What? I thought we were riding together." More silence. "Well you should just tell him you're leaving the car in long term parking."

The conversation went back and forth for a few more minutes. Her stomach clenched when she heard Gary say, "I love you, and I can't wait to see you. Good-bye for now, I'll see you on the plane." He hung up.

Not willing to allow Gary to see her, Tanya rushed to Cassandra's room and quietly closed the door.

By the time Tanya woke the next morning, Gary was gone. She peered into their bedroom and spied the contents of his closet strewn all over the floor. Immediately she rushed to her dresser and pulled the drawer open where she had hidden the manila envelope. She let out a sigh of relief, grabbed the envelope and ran down stairs.

Tanya thumbed through the paid bills and came across the recent phone bill. After scanning the numbers, she found one that had been used during the day while she had been at work. *Long distance calls are great.* She thought as she jotted down the number on the envelope. It was after nine before she gathered the courage to dial the number.

A somber male voice came over the line. "Hello?"

Tanya sucked in a deep breath. "Is this Mr. Wilkins?"

"Yes, who may I ask is calling?"

"My name is Tanya Antonio; I have information concerning your wife."

Tanya heard him suck in a deep breath. "Believe it or not, I was going to call you today. If you're married to Gary, I think we have the same problem."

"I am, and I really think we should get together….how about two thirty this afternoon? I think have some information to share."

There was a brief pause. "Do you think my wife and your husband are having an affair?"

"I do, and I have the proof. As I said before, I'll share this information with you this afternoon."

"I'll be here…I'll see you around two thirty." After giving Tanya the address, he hung up.

Tanya parked in front of an older Victorian home on a narrow street in a city fifteen miles from her home. She stared down at the scrap of paper with Mr. Wilkins' address, sighed and climbed out of the car. She wondered what the man was going to say when she presented him with the pile of paperwork. Her heart wasn't broken, but she knew he was very upset when they spoke on the phone.

The front door flew open before Tanya had a chance to knock. "Mrs. Antonio?"

A tall thin man with sandy brown hair and dark eyes stood in the doorway. His eyes were red and puffy the telltale sign he had been crying. Tanya extended her hand. "Please, call me Tanya."

He grasped her hand firmly and led her inside. He stood beside a long dining room table that donned a white lace cloth. The room seemed tiny in comparison to the size table. "Have a seat." He said as he held out his arm. "My name is Michael...Mike."

Tanya placed the large envelope on the table and sat. Mike stared down at the envelope and his eyes welled with tears. She stared up at him and said, "I think you'd better sit down, I can tell by the look on your face this affair has hurt you. I really don't like being the bearer of bad news, but I feel you have a right to know what's been going on."

Mike pulled out a chair, rested his arms on the table and laced his fingers. "Do you have any idea how long this has been going on?"

"From what I can gather, it started about two and a half, maybe three years ago."

"That's what I thought." A tear trickled down his sad face. Embarrassed, Mike quickly brushed it away with a sweep of his hand. "I'm sorry; you must think I'm a big cry baby."

Tanya smiled. "Not at all, I can see you're a man who loves his wife. I know you're in pain, and just to let you know, it's alright for a man to cry." Tanya opened the flap of the envelope and slowly removed its contents. "These are the cards and receipts my husband saved over the course of their affair. Apparently Samantha has confessed her love to my husband...numerous times."

Mike couldn't hold back his tears. He grasped one of the cards and stared down at his wife's handwriting. He ran a finger over the words. "She used to send me cards and love notes." He returned the card to the pile and lifted a receipt. After reading the description he looked into Tanya's eyes and said, "This receipt is for the necklace she's been wearing for the last few years. When I questioned her about it, she said she bought it one day when she was shopping with a friend. I guess that friend was your husband."

Tanya tried to comfort the grieving man. "Mike, I can tell by looking at you, your wife means the world to you."

"He sniffed and dried his tears. His eyes became stone cold. "We were high school sweethearts. We've been married a little over eleven years." He clenched his jaw. "I can't forgive her for this. I refuse to live with a woman who can take my heart and toss it out the window like it's some kind of worthless trash. I do love her, but I can't stay with her…" His voice turned raspy.

Tanya placed a gentle hand on his forearm. "I know you're hurting, but in time I'm sure you can find a way to forgive her."

He glared at her. "I'm not staying with her. I'll be filing for divorce first thing Monday morning. She's carried on this affair for years and I'm through." He looked at her for a long moment. "Can I ask you a question?" Tanya nodded. "Why isn't this bothering you? I mean you're sitting here with all this evidence and you seem to be…taking it very well."

"My marriage has been over for quite some time. To be completely honest, I never loved my husband…" She stared into his eyes. "I married him because I was pregnant and my mother said it was the right thing to do. I'm going to tell you one thing; my husband is not a nice man. He's degrading and argumentative. He'll take your wife and belittle her in months. He has no compassion for anyone. The only thing I can say, I was waiting for another affair to give me an excuse to end the marriage."

Mike was shocked. "You mean he's cheated on you before…why did you stay?"

Tanya shrugged. "Fear mostly. I don't know when I'll leave, but it'll be soon." She rose to her feet, slid the envelope to Mike while saying, "You keep this. I'm sure once your wife sees you have ammunition; she'll give you what you want. My only suggestion would be, make copies and show her the copies...make sure she doesn't get her hands on this stuff." Tanya patted the envelope.

Mike grinned for the first time. "She won't fight me once she sees she doesn't have a leg to stand on." Realization crossed his handsome face. "What are you going to use? I mean if you're giving me this stuff how..."

"Don't worry about me. You need this to take her for the ride she's been waiting for. I have enough to get what I want."

"If you don't mind me asking, what do you want?"

Tanya smiled. "My kids."

Mike scoffed. "Samantha hates kids...how many do you have?"

"I have two. One's sixteen and one's five. I can't understand why, a woman who hates kids, would go for a man that has two."

"I'm sure she never thought about it. If I was to guess, I'd say she never thought she'd get caught."

Tanya left the sorrowful man and climbed into her car. As she drove along the interstate she wondered if she had done the right thing. She stared out the windshield and admired the few remaining leaves on the trees. She wondered if she would have the strength to divorce Gary and if she did where would she go.

Gary came home two weeks later acting like nothing had happened. He smiled when he walked through the door with gifts. "Daddy's home." He bellowed. "I bought gifts for my three favorite people."

Cassandra screeched when she heard his voice. Jason remained on the sofa playing video games. Gary scowled when no one greeted him. Tanya was walking down the stairs when she noticed him. Her stomach immediately clenched and the all too familiar pains shot up her chest. The coppery taste she had grown accustomed to was the early warning sign of the blood she would spew later. "Oh, hi Gary, I didn't hear you come in."

Gary glared at her. "What did you do? The kids won't even come to say hello."

"I didn't do anything."

Immediately Gary lashed out and started yelling. Tanya ran back up the stairs and into the bathroom. She closed the door just in time for the contents of her stomach to erupt into the toilet. Blood mixed the undigested food from lunch; the pains she felt brought her to her knees. After a few long moments she wiped her mouth, brushed her teeth and walked downstairs.

"I'm sorry." Gary said as soon as he heard her enter the kitchen. "I love you. I didn't mean to come home and treat you like that."

Tanya reached into the cabinet for a glass. "I'm used to it."

"That's no excuse. I should learn to be a little nicer." The phone rang and Gary rushed to answer it. "Hello?"

The silence was killing Tanya. She knew Samantha was on the other end just by the way Gary's body stiffened. "Yes I'm home."

Tanya stared at his back. *Wow she barely waited long enough for him to get in the door before she called him…that's love for you.*

Gary slammed down the phone an entered the kitchen. The rage in his eyes caused Tanya to take two steps back. "Thanks to you and your fucking nosiness, Samantha and her husband are getting divorced. You had no right to give him my shit. I have a good mind to divorce you for this little fiasco."

Tanya walked past him and entered the living room. She spied Cassandra behind the sofa with her hands over her ears. She was crying. After coaxing her daughter from her hidden position something snapped inside Tanya. It was the very moment she spied her child hiding behind the sofa when she realized something had to give. The arguing had to stop.

"Shhh baby, everything's all right."

Cassandra said through her sobs, "No it's not…daddy's yelling."

Tanya kissed her daughter and held her for a few long moments. Once the ranting and raving had ceased Cassandra relaxed and fell asleep. Carrying her daughter up the stairs, Tanya made her final decision.

The next morning Gary woke in a chipper mood. He had no idea Cassandra was bothered by his arguing, as a matter of fact he acted like nothing happened. "Tanya sweetheart, our anniversary is coming up in a couple of weeks…what would you like?"

Tanya smiled. "A divorce."

Gary laughed. "That's a good one. Seriously, if you don't tell me, then I'll just have to figure out something." She shrugged and the conversation ended.

Two weeks later, Gary handed her a small package, gave her a kiss and said, "Happy anniversary I hope you like it."

Tanya opened the jeweler's box and spied a gold necklace. Knowing he had never given her jewelry in the past, Tanya was at a loss for words. "Thank you." She said softly.

He smiled and asked, "So what would you like for Christmas?"

With tears in her eyes and the box in her hand she simply said, "A divorce and you're paying for it." After placing the box on the table Tanya rose to her feet and walked out of the room.

It was just after six p.m. on Christmas Eve when a knock came on the door. Tanya

entered the foyer and swung open the door. A
sheriff stood on the porch with a solemn look
on his face. "Tanya Antonio?"

"Yes." She had a confused look on her
face when the man handed her a few sheets of
papers.

"I'm sorry to have to do this on
Christmas Eve, but you've been served."

She smiled knowing, even before she
looked at the papers what they were. "Oh no,
you don't have to be sorry. I wanted this."

The man nodded and gave her a
halfhearted smile. "Have a Merry Christmas
was all he said as he turned and stepped
across the porch.

Gary approached Tanya a month after
the divorce papers had been delivered. He had
a menacing look in his eyes. He said, "I
should kill you. You're taking everything away
from me. I love you and all you want to do is
get a divorce. I won't have my kids I won't
have the woman I love… I should fucking kill
you."

She smiled even though her heart was
beating erratically. Fear was consuming her.
She stared back and said, "Dead or divorced
I'll be rid of you." She pushed past him and
entered the kitchen.

Gary growled, "I'll give you your divorce,
because in time, I know we'll end up back
together…"

She chuckled when she heard those words. *Don't count on it.* She thought

Five months later Tanya sat on the witness stand in a dimly lit courtroom. She stared into the solemn face of her husband. The judge said to Tanya, "If you'd like to hire an attorney we can postpone the proceedings."

Tanya pulled her eyes away from Gary and stared up at the judge. "No ma'am, I'll be divorced today."

She returned her stare to Gary. The judge scowled at him. "I don't know what the hell you did to this woman, but you'd better consider yourself lucky she didn't hire an attorney. Frankly, if she fought for anything, I would have given it to her. You must be a real piece or work Mr. Antonio." The judge slammed down her gavel and said. "Case closed."

A huge weight lifted off Tanya's chest. Seventeen and a half years of being tormented was finally over. She grinned as she signed the paperwork, and thought, *now my life will begin.*

Epilogue

It's been fifteen years since Tanya's and Gary's divorce was finalized. Although life has been rough for her, it's been easy in comparison to the life she lived with Gary.

Gary lives with Samantha in the house where Tanya had lived. She smiles whenever she hears about the disrespectful way Samantha treats him. He's stuck in relationship where he gets badgered. She's thankful for the way her life turned out. Although she's not married and has no intention to ever get into that situation again, Tanya is free. Just knowing she can enter her house without hearing ridicule is a blessing.

The words I love you to this day causes Tanya to cringe. She has warned the men she's dated, if they never said those words, everything would be perfect. Tanya has left a couple of nice men because they said those words. She swears if she ever hears those three words roll off a man's tongue, it would be too soon.

The kids have grown as kids do. Jason has left the nest and has become a very successful program designer. Cassandra remains with her mother and rarely sees her father. She despises the way Gary has treated her in the past, and at this point in her life, she feels holidays are about all she can stand.

Tanya's personal motto, "A bad day outside of my marriage marriage is far better than the best day in the marriage."

About the Author

Valerie Bowen lives with her son in Connecticut. She is the author of the For the Sake of Amelia series and the Mind of a Madman series

****

Follow Valerie on the web:

Websites:
http://www.valeriebowen.com
http://www.opusnpen.com

E-mail:
val2262001@yahoo.com

Facebook:
https://www.facebook.com/pages/Author-Valerie-Bowen

Printed in Great Britain
by Amazon